The
Myth
and
Madness
of
Ophelia

Frontispiece (Figure 24)
EDWARD STEICHEN
Lillian Gish (1893–1993) as Ophelia, 1936
Gelatin silver print
The Museum of Modern Art, New York
Gift of the Photographer
Reprinted with permission of Joanna T. Steichen

The Myth and Madness of Ophelia

Carol Solomon Kiefer

Contributions by

Georgianna Ziegler

H. R. Coursen

Foreword by

Jill Meredith

Mead Art Museum

Amherst College

Amherst, Massachusetts

2001

This catalogue is published in conjunction with the exhibition *The Myth and Madness of Ophelia*, which was organized by the Mead Art Museum. Publication support was provided by the Hall and Kate Peterson Fund and the Charles H. Morgan Fund.

Mead Art Museum
Amherst College
Amherst, Massachusetts
October 26–December 16, 2001

Library of Congress Cataloging-in-Publication Data

The myth and madness of Ophelia/edited by Carol Solomon Kiefer with contributions by Georgianna Ziegler and H. R. Coursen; foreword by Jill Meredith.
     p. cm.
   Catalogue of an exhibition held at the Mead Art Museum, Amherst College, Amherst, Mass., October 26-December 16, 2001.
   Includes bibliographical references.
   ISBN 0-914337-24-6
     1. Ophelia (Fictitious character) in art—Exhibitions. 2. Shakespeare, William, 1564–1616—Characters—Ophelia—Exhibitions. 3. Arts, Modern—Exhibitions. I. Kiefer, Carol Solomon—II. Mead Art Museum (Amherst College)

NX652.O64 M98 2001
700'.451—dc21   2001044389

Cover: Francis Legat after **Benjamin West**
Detail of *Hamlet. Act IV, scene v. Elsinore. –King, Queen, Laertes, Ophelia, & c.,* 1802
Engraving
Amherst College
Archives and Special Collections
Photo: Stephen Petegorsky
(Figure 5)

Designed by Su Auerbach
Printed by Thames Printing Co. Inc., Norwich, Connecticut

Contents

Foreword

The Myth and Madness of Ophelia—both the exhibition and this volume of critical essays and installation checklist—surveys the multiple interpretations of Shakespeare's heroine in the visual and performing arts since the eighteenth century. The dramatic readings by theater's and film's most illustrious actresses have been inspired by, and, in turn, inspired the profusion of paintings, prints, drawings, and photographs depicting *Hamlet's* Ophelia. Although a minor character in the play, her madness and death (which occurs offstage) gave rise to a feminine mythology about her character, which has mirrored cultural concerns and mores.

In contemporary society, Ophelia has been appropriated as a feminist and post-feminist icon. Whether a psychological metaphor for female adolescents at risk of emotional damage by patriarchal society (*Reviving Ophelia* and *Ophelia Speaks*), a pop diva's musical theme (Natalie Merchant's 1998 CD *Ophelia*) or the petal-strewn self-portrait of photographer Charlotta Westergren (Dee/ Glasoe Gallery, August 2001 exhibition *Heroine*)—to name just a few recent examples—the myth of Ophelia continues to accrue relevance and significance to modern women.

In this unique project, curator Carol Solomon Kiefer delved into the rich literary, dramatic, dance, and artistic traditions of the past two and a half centuries to provide an overview and the many, intertwined interpretations starting with artworks in the collection of the Mead Art Museum. To demonstrate the continuing presence of Ophelia in contemporary art, particularly by women artists, Kiefer dipped into the stream of imagery to present works overtly depicting Ophelia by Louise Bourgeois and Linda Stark as well as the more evocative images by photographers Mary Ellen Mark and Leeanne Schmidt. Her essay in this volume outlines the many literary, artistic, performative, intellectual, and psychological aspects that comprise the complex figure of Ophelia. I am grateful to my colleague, Carol Solomon Kiefer, for pursuing this topic with such enthusiasm, erudition, and imagination. As we bring *Ophelia* to Amherst, we have sent our own daughters off to college—I thank her too for such good friendship in this.

The Folger Shakespeare Library in Washington, D.C., provided the greatest number of loan works from its renowned collection of illustrated books, prints, photographs, paintings, and literary ephemera. Indeed, this project is a major collaboration between these two cultural institutions and highlights the historic association between Amherst College and the Folger Shakespeare Library. This project was exceptional for the Folger and its staff, and we deeply appreciate their efforts to accommodate the substantial loan request. We are indebted especially to Werner Gundersheimer (Amherst College, Class of 1959), Director, and Richard Kuhta, Librarian, for their unstinting cooperation and support. The other institutional lenders, artists, dealers, and private collectors who have provided artworks as well as information, photographs, and reproduction rights are gratefully acknowledged for their contributions. Their generosity makes possible a more diverse exhibition and catalogue.

The contributions of essayists and Shakespeare specialists, Georgianna Ziegler of the Folger Shakespeare Library, and H. R. Coursen (Amherst College, Class of 1954) of the University of Maine, Augusta, enriched this project throughout. Ziegler's 1997 Folger exhibition and catalogue *Shakespeare's Unruly Women* was a source of inspiration for the present project. She writes here about the Victorian spiritualization of Ophelia. H. R. Coursen, a widely published scholar, considers the actresses who have played the part of Ophelia in modern films and stage productions.

We are grateful, also, to the Hall and Kate Peterson Fund and the Charles H. Morgan Fund for financial support of this exhibition and publication, without which the many loans and handsome production of the volume would not have been possible.

Jill Meredith
Director and Curator of European Art
Mead Art Museum
Amherst College

Acknowledgments

In preparing *The Myth and Madness of Ophelia* exhibition, its catalogue, and related programs, I have relied on many people — scholars, artists, museum professionals, dealers, private collectors, friends, and others — and I have drawn on the resources of numerous institutions.

First and foremost, I would like to acknowledge the contributions of Georgianna Ziegler of the Folger Shakespeare Library and H. R. Coursen (Amherst College, Class of 1954) of the University of Maine, Augusta. I have benefited greatly from their knowledge, encouragement, and generosity of spirit. I am especially indebted to Werner Gundersheimer (Amherst College, Class of 1959), Director of the Folger, Richard Kuhta, Librarian, and the staff of the Folger, who worked so hard to accommodate the many demands implicit in a loan of this size. In particular, I would like to mention the cooperation and professional kindnesses extended by Georgianna Ziegler, Rachel Doggett, Erin Blake, J. Franklin Mowery, Julie Ainsworth, and Deborah J. Leslie.

I would like to thank the institutional lenders to the exhibition as well as Margaret and Henry Erbe, artists, dealers, the anonymous private collector, and others who loaned works, assisted in arranging loans, or provided photographs for the show and the catalogue. In particular, I would like to express my gratitude to Louise Bourgeois for making her print available for acquisition and for the assistance of Wendy Williams in facilitating its purchase. Nancy Allison, who has been extremely generous with her time and assistance, made the video and photographs of Jean Erdman's *Ophelia* available. Lilli-Mari Andresen of Angles Gallery in Santa Monica arranged for the loan of *Ophelia Forever* by Linda Stark, who kindly provided background information and a statement regarding the meaning of her work.

Many other individuals provided valuable assistance of one form or another. Among them are: Clifford Ackley, Charleen Alcid, Michael Almereyda, Mary Clare Altenhofen, Amanda Bowen, Victor Burgin, Sheron Burton, James Conlin, Gregory Crewdson, Linda-Anne D'Anjou, Janis Eckdahl, Gil Einstein, Margit Erb, Annette Fern, Olivia Lahs-Gonzales, Heather Haskell, Claudel Huot, Robert Herbert, Michael Kiefer, Zoe Kiefer, Susan Kismaric, Natalia Mager, Mary Ellen Mark, Patrick Murphy, Weston Naef, Sue Reed, Jennifer Roberts, Ronald Rosbottom, Leeanne Schmidt, Elizabeth Solomon, Alice Steinhardt, Stephanie Stepanek, Julie Sweiden, Frank Trapp, Scott Wilcox, Liz Ziegler, Christine Burgin Gallery, Luhring Augustine Gallery, and Howard Greenberg Gallery.

I would like to thank the staff of the Robert Frost Library at Amherst College, especially Daria D'Arienzo, Susan Lisk, Tracy Sutherland, Michael Kasper, and John Kunhardt. The catalogue was designed by Su Auerbach, with whom it has been a pleasure to work. Douglas Wilson, College Editor, kindly read and commented on the manuscript. Photography was provided by Frank Ward, Stephen Petegorsky, and Diane Gray.

Last, but not least, I acknowledge the invaluable contributions made by my colleagues at the Mead Art Museum: Donna Abelli, Karen Cardinal, Trinkett Clark, Stephen Fisher, Tim Gilfillan, Martha Hoppin, and Karen Suchenski. A special note of thanks goes to Allison Sobke, graduate intern from the University of Massachusetts, Amherst, who energetically assisted in all aspects of the preparation of the catalogue and exhibition. Finally, I would like to express my gratitude to Jill Meredith, Director of the Mead, for her continued support and assistance.

Carol Solomon Kiefer
Visiting Curator
Mead Art Museum
Amherst College

Lenders to the Exhibition

Nancy Allison, New York

Margaret and Henry Erbe

Private Collection, Glendale, California

Archives and Special Collections, Amherst College

Ex Machina, Quebec City, Quebec

Fine Arts Library, Harvard University

Folger Shakespeare Library, Washington, D.C.

George Eastman House

Harry Ransom Humanities Research Center, The University of Texas at Austin

The Montreal Museum of Fine Arts

Museum of Fine Arts, Boston

Museum of Fine Arts, Springfield, Massachusetts

The Museum of Modern Art, New York

The Museum of Modern Art Library, New York

Photofest, New York

The Royal Society of Medicine, London, England

The Saint Louis Art Museum

Yale Center for British Art

poor Ophelia

Divided from herself and her fair judgment,

Without the which we are pictures, or mere beasts;

—Claudius
Hamlet (Act IV, scene 5)

Figure 1
THOMAS FRANCIS DICKSEE
Ophelia, 1875
Oil on canvas
Mead Art Museum
Museum Purchase
1961.4
Photo: Stephen Petegorsky

The Myth and Madness of Ophelia

Carol Solomon Kiefer

There is a willow grows askant the brook
That shows his hoary leaves in the glassy stream.
Therewith fantastic garlands did she make
Of crow-flowers, nettles, daisies, and long purples,
That liberal shepherds give a grosser name,
But our cold maids do dead men's fingers call them.
There on the pendent boughs her crownet weeds
Clamb'ring to hang, an envious sliver broke,
When down her weedy trophies and herself
Fell in the weeping brook. Her clothes spread wide,
And mermaid-like awhile they bore her up,
Which time she chanted snatches of old lauds,
As one incapable of her own distress,
Or like a creature native and indued
Unto that element. But long it could not be
Til that her garments, heavy with their drink,
Pull'd the poor wretch from her melodious lay
To muddy death.
           Hamlet (Act IV, scene 7, 165-182)[1]

he death of Ophelia, recounted by Hamlet's mother, Gertrude, Queen of Denmark, is an offstage event in Shakespeare's play, but the Bard's verse is easily visualized. Paradoxically, we see and feel beauty in the awful reality of a troubled girl's death by drowning. The scene has a long history of visual representation, beginning in the eighteenth century and continuing to the present. Ophelia is the most frequently depicted of Shakespeare's heroines and certainly one of the most popular and intriguing of all his characters. But it is more than Shakespeare's poetry and the universal fascination with death that accounts for Ophelia's popularity. Hers is the sentimental tale of a victim, young and beautiful. She is an especially intriguing character, however, because of her madness — a madness that is intimately linked to her femininity.

The cause of Ophelia's madness is unclear, an ambiguity surely intended by Shakespeare. Was it the result of her rejected love, the death of her father, or a combination of the two? Doubt also lingers about the precise circumstances of her death. Was it an accidental drowning, as reported by Gertrude, or was it suicide, as implied by the gravedigger (Act V, scene 1)? These ambiguities add to the mystique of Ophelia.

Mythologized over time, Ophelia has attained the status of a cult figure, appropriated in popular culture to such an extent that she has become a cliché. Today, her name is used to market a range of products from bed linens ("Ophelia Bed in Bag" by Dan River) to patterns of china.[2] In recent book titles (*Reviving Ophelia; Ophelia Speaks; Ophelia's Mom),* she has emerged as the symbol of the adolescent girl in search of self.[3] "Ophelia" is the title track of Natalie Merchant's recent *Ophelia* CD; its slipcase shows the artist in a number of roles, including the madwoman. "How to Create an Ophelia Costume" is featured on the *e How to…* Website, where ten "how to" steps rehearse the standard Ophelia iconography and promise that "you will feel just like one of Shakespeare's most tragic heroines in this Ophelia (after the drowning) costume."[4] Numerous other Websites devoted to Ophelia (many serious and scholarly) document her presence, her power, her relevance, and her unending chain of signification in contemporary life. Diana, Princess of Wales, who fit the Ophelia archetype, was a beloved present-day incarnation of the Shakespearean character, whose tragic undoing fascinated the world.

The image of Ophelia, to borrow the language of Barthes, "is constituted by an architecture of signs drawn from a variable depth of lexicons. . . entering into mutual relations of dialogue, parody, contestation, but there is one place where this multiplicity is focused and that is the reader."[5] Ophelia in any representation is a site of memory, fantasy, projection, and desire. Although she continually takes on new forms because she is what one brings to her, Ophelia is embedded or encoded with a specific set of distinguishing characteristics and meanings.

Iconographically, Ophelia most often appears as young and beautiful, although she can have a wan, frail look, with a consumptive-like pallor. She often has a lost gaze, a sign of her madness. Her long, disheveled hair is often strewn with flowers or twigs and straw, which may be shaped in the form of a garland. She sometimes carries or distributes flowers, which have various symbolic meanings. Ophelia usually wears a long flowing white dress, a sign of her purity and innocence. However, she is sometimes bare-breasted, an indication of her sensuality and eroticism. A cloak is sometimes draped around her shoulders. She is linked with water and is often depicted at the side of or floating in a stream.

A secondary character in Shakespeare's most famous play, Ophelia was until the second half of the twentieth century treated summarily in the critical literature. In the last few decades, however, she has become the subject of intense analysis, largely by scholars with a feminist or psychoanalytic perspective, who have introduced new ways of interpreting her character. Once seen only as a pathetic, innocent, submissive, and dutiful daughter, sister, and lover, Ophelia is now also perceived as a figure of strength, a heroine whose madness is seen as an assertion of self, an act of rebellion against patriarchal control. Recent studies of Ophelia's visual representation use a variety of critical and socio-historical approaches. Images of the Shakespearean heroine are inscribed in discourses relating to the concept of femininity, to notions of ideal womanhood, to the historically gendered understanding of madness as a female malady, and to the very idea of representation itself.[6] Although a subject of international artistic appeal, Ophelia, not surprisingly, has been most frequently represented in British art. In England, during the nineteenth century, images of Ophelia appeared in the exhibitions of the Royal Academy no less than fifty times. According to Richard Altick, the theme was the single most represented subject of English literary painting.[7]

The image of Ophelia cast specifically as "a document in madness" (Laertes's description of his sister in Act IV, scene 5) is established early in the history of her representation. The wild, emotional, and erotic visual representations of her insanity become more pronounced in the nineteenth century under the sway of Romanticism. They were not, however, absent in the late eighteenth century, although images of that time often understate or even suppress her distracted condition. These representations reflect an idealized conception of the pure and innocent Ophelia, a sentimentally precious, aesthetic object, bereft of sexuality and pitiful in her frail, delicate madness.

To Samuel Johnson in 1765, Ophelia was "the young, the beautiful, the harmless, and the pious."[8] Francis Hayman's drawing of the play scene (Act III, scene 2) (fig. 2) of around 1740–41, one of the first pictorial appearances of Ophelia, exemplifies Johnson's sense of the character. In this work, engraved by Hubert Gravelot and published in 1744 as the frontispiece to *Hamlet* in one of the early illustrated editions of Shakespeare's works, there is little suggestion of Ophelia's incipient madness other than her lost gaze. Another early representation, an etching by Daniel Berger after Daniel Nikolaus Chodowiecki's drawing of 1778 (fig. 3), shows Ophelia with downcast eyes, the proper, lady-like figure of eighteenth-century restraint and decorum. Representing her mad scene (Act IV, scene 5), Thomas Stothard's delicately rendered *Ophelia* (fig. 4) of 1783 adheres to the same stereotype of ideal femininity and refinement. Were it not for Laertes's gesture of despair and the stunned reactions of the King, Queen, and their attendants, it would be hard to ascertain that the sweet young girl distributing flowers in this picture is mad. Stothard's Ophelia echoes the norms of late eighteenth-century stage productions of *Hamlet*, in which the more bawdy aspects of her character were censored.

Benjamin West depicts the same scene (fig. 5) and unmasks Ophelia's unraveled state of mind. First commissioned for exhibition in the Boydell Shakespeare Gallery, the 1792 painting was engraved in 1802 by Francis Legat for sale as a print.[9] The action focuses on Ophelia, the cause of the visible anguish and discomfort of all present. Strong highlights pull the viewer's eye to her ample thigh and belly — to her womanhood. Barefooted, wild eyes framed by disheveled locks of hair and straw, her dress billows with the movements of her crazed dance. She is the image of uncontrolled madness.

The same frenzied, unanchored woman is captured in Francesco Bartolozzi's etching after Henry Tresham's 1794 *Ophelia vide Hamlet* (fig. 6). Breasts bared, hair

Figure 2
FRANCIS HAYMAN
The Play Scene from **Hamlet**
[Act III, scene 2], c. 1740–1741
Pen and ink and wash
By Permission of the Folger
Shakespeare Library

Figure 3
DANIEL BERGER
After drawing of 1778
by DANIEL NIKOLAUS
CHODOWIECKI
Die Mausfalle. **Hamlet**.
*III. Aufsug 2ter Auftritt
[The Mousetrap,* **Hamlet**,
Act III, Sc. 2], 1780
Etching
By Permission of the
Folger Shakespeare
Library

OPHELIA.

There's fennel for you, and columbines. There's rue for you.

Vid. Shakespeare Hamlet

London, Published Octr. 25. 1783. by Thos. Macklin, No. 39 Fleet Street.

Figure 4
JOHN OGBORNE, THE ELDER
After **THOMAS STOTHARD**
Ophelia, 1783
Etching, engraving and aquatint printed in light brown
By Permission of the Folger Shakespeare Library

Figure 5
FRANCIS LEGAT
After painting of 1792
by BENJAMIN WEST
Hamlet. *Act IV, scene v.*
Elsinore.–King, Queen,
Laertes, Ophelia, & c., 1802
Engraving
Amherst College
Archives and Special
Collections
Photo: Stephen Petegorsky

Figure 6
FRANCESCO BARTOLOZZI
After drawing by HENRY TRESHAM
Ophelia vide Hamlet, 1794
Colored etching
By Permission of the Folger Shakespeare Library

Figure 7
JOHN HAMILTON MORTIMER
Ophelia (Act IV, scene 7), 1775
Black charcoal drawing
By Permission of the Folger Shakespeare Library

flying, her gaze otherworldly, Ophelia reaches precariously to hang her garland of flowers on a willow branch as three female onlookers on the opposite bank gesture in awful anticipation of her tragedy. No evidence of flattery or idealization is found in the Ophelia of John Hamilton Mortimer's 1775 portrait of madness (fig. 7), one in a series of twelve "Heads" featuring Shakespearean characters.

These few late eighteenth-century examples convey how varied the presentation of Ophelia's afflicted state of mind was in the early phase of her representation. As Mary Floyd-Wilson has remarked, "Rather than merely presenting a one-dimensional, 'decorous and pious' character, the eighteenth century conceived of an amalgam of ambiguities. 'Ophelia' did the cultural work of yoking together passivity and femininity, sexual innocence and sexual appeal, and emotionality and vulnerability."[10] Visually, madness became the defining trait of Ophelia's character, and it continued to be a major focus of representations of her.

In the nineteenth century, as argued by Elaine Showalter, madness was identified with femininity. Ophelia became a prototype for the insane woman, a model for its clinical diagnosis and for the first photographic documentation of female insanity.[11] One of the key figures contributing to this evolution was Dr. Hugh Welch Diamond (1809–1886), the resident medical superintendent of female patients at the Surrey County Lunatic Asylum at Springfield and a pioneering figure in the history of photography. In a series of rare public exhibitions, beginning in 1852, he showed photographs he had taken of his patients. Originally exhibited as "the Types of Insanity," these portraits represent the first use of photography in the clinical practice of psychiatry. They were intended to document correlations between physiognomic characteristics and various types of mental illness. In 1858, lithographic illustrations based on Diamond's photographs were used by one of the leading psychiatrists of the day, John Conolly, in a series of important essays on "The Physiognomy of Insanity."[12]

One of Diamond's photographs represents a type of female hysteria, a lovesick suicidal insanity, then also known as erotomania (fig. 8). The seated young woman is self-protective in bearing and expression. Through Diamond's creative intervention, she literally assumes the mantle of Ophelia: he draped her in a cloak and placed a garland of flowers in her hair. The presence of these recognizable props served only to enhance identification of the type. Victorian psychiatrists universally

acknowledged Shakespeare as a reliable aid in diagnosing the many "Ophelia types" entrusted to their care. John Conolly, not unique among psychiatrists as a writer on Shakespeare, wrote an 1863 *Study of Hamlet* praising the realism of Ophelia's characterization. "Never did poet's pen draw so touching and so true a portrait of madness fallen on a delicate and affectionate girl," stated Conolly.[13] "Our asylums for ruined minds now and then present remarkable illustrations of the

Figure 8
HUGH WELCH DIAMOND
Untitled [Mental Patient, Surrey County Lunatic Asylum]
Copy of original albumen print, c. 1851–52
By kind permission of the Royal Society of Medicine, London, England

fatal malady," he wrote, "so that even casual visitors recognize in the wards an Ophelia; the same young years, the same faded beauty, the same fantastic dress and interrupted song."[14] In 1859, Dr. Charles Bucknill, president of the Medico-Psychological Association, wrote that "Ophelia is the very type of a class of cases by no means uncommon. Every mental physician of

Figure 9
Miss Ellen Terry (1847–1928) as Ophelia, 1878–1904
Carte-de-visite photograph
By Permission of the Folger Shakespeare Library

Figure 10
ANNA MASSEY LEA MERRITT
Ophelia, 1880
Etching
Gift of Sylvester Rosa Koehler, K1617
Courtesy, Museum of Fine Arts, Boston
Reproduced with Permission
© 2000 Museum of Fine Arts, Boston. All Rights Reserved

moderately extensive experience must have seen many Ophelias. It is a copy from nature, after the fashion of the Pre-Raphaelites."[15]

Extending this circle of literature and art informing life and medical practice, Conolly, in 1863, recommended that actresses "might find the contemplation of such cases a not unprofitable study,"[16] and they followed his advice. Of the role that contributed so much to her fame, the great Ellen Terry (fig. 9) remarked almost twenty years later, "Like all Ophelias before (and after) me, I went to the madhouse to study wits astray."[17] But, as Showalter explains, the affectation of Ophelian traits by truly mad women was by this time so pronounced that Terry denied the value of the experience, claiming that reality was "too *theatrical*."[18] For others, however, including visual artists, it was still considered a worthwhile pursuit.

In 1879, the American expatriate painter and printmaker Anna Lea Merritt was commissioned to do an etched portrait of Ellen Terry, who was then playing the role of Ophelia. Merritt observed Terry in performance, but in fulfilling the commission she was obliged to sacrifice the actress's convincing emotional portrayal of Ophelia's madness in order to provide the truest likeness of Terry.[19] Determined "to make a painting of Ophelia really mad," Merritt gained access to "Bedlam" [Bethlem] Hospital in search of a *real* model.[20] One patient, encountered in the garden, provided the inspiration for her 1880 painting and the etching that followed (fig. 10). The artist observed:

> . . . a lovely young woman, picking up odds and ends as she slowly walked. Then she dropped on her knees, continuing to move, kneeling and grasping against her breast the bundles she had gathered — faded flowers, torn bits of paper, dead leaves, a reel of cotton! Just in front of us she stopped, looking full in my eyes with an expression questioning, doubtful, full of pain. Suddenly she grasped my skirt and said, "Kiss me." I kissed her forehead and then hastily turned to be led away. Something of her expression I got into my picture. It was hung on the line in the [Royal] Academy.[21]

In search of compelling content for her Ophelia, Merritt turned not to Shakespeare's text or to the great Ellen Terry, but rather to the dramatic confines of a mental hospital. The result is a confounding of fact and fiction — a wistful, beautiful, ultimately romanticized conception of the Shakespearean heroine.

Historically, the representation of Ophelia's death has been as captivating as the representation of her madness. It is the subject of the most famous image of Ophelia, the 1851–52 painting by the Pre-Raphaelite artist John Everett Millais (fig. 11), a postcard favorite of visitors to the Tate Gallery in London. This painting has itself served as the source for many depictions of the subject, several of which are discussed here and included in the exhibition.

Relying closely on Shakespeare's text, the work shows the scene of Ophelia's drowning as narrated by Gertrude (Act IV, scene 7). However, Millais's presentation of Ophelia in the water, in the final act of drowning, slowly drifting to her death, was a departure from the usual treatment of the scene. Traditionally, Ophelia appears *before* her fateful fall standing or sitting on the bank of the brook, as in Thomas Francis Dicksee's wan and consumptive *Ophelia* of 1875 (fig. 1), or leaning toward the water attempting to hang a garland of flowers on a willow branch, as in Richard Westall's iconographically influential painting of 1793 (fig. 12).[22] Another variant is Jules-Joseph Lefebvre's 1890 oil on canvas, from the Springfield Museum of Fine Arts, in which an entranced Ophelia stands calmly in the still waters of a quiet brook surrounded by reeds and lily pads (fig. 53). Most rare is the depiction of Ophelia dead, as in the painting by the French artist James Bertrand, exhibited at the Paris Salon of 1872 and illustrated as a drawing after the painting in an 1884 issue of the French art magazine *L'Artiste* (fig. 13). Two courtiers in a boat pull the lifeless body of Ophelia from the water under the light of the moon. Gertrude does not describe such a scene; in fact the retrieval of Ophelia's body is nowhere described in Shakespeare's text.

In choosing to render the actual drowning, Millais was preceded by Eugène Delacroix, the French artist who most fully embraced the character of Ophelia. Under the spell of the emotionally vivid performances of Irish actress Harriet Smithson in the late 1820s (figs. 14, 15), Delacroix was one of a generation of French Romantics who made of Ophelia "a cult figure embodying their own turbulent hopes."[23] Nina Auerbach writes that "for Berlioz [who married Smithson, so captivated was he by her Ophelia], Hugo, and Delacroix, Ophelia swelled into a magic symbol of an erotic and aesthetic awakening that soared far beyond her ancillary role in Shakespeare's play."[24] Throughout the nineteenth century and beyond, Ophelia continued to captivate the French literary and artistic imagination. For Baudelaire, she was conceived as Hamlet's "specular counterpart. . . .whose engulfment and regenerative death in a Lethe-like stream served as an enticing

Figure 11
JOHN EVERETT MILLAIS
Ophelia, 1851–52
Oil on canvas
Tate Gallery, London
Copyright Tate Gallery, London/Art Resource, NY

Figure 12
RICHARD WESTALL
*Ophelia (**Hamlet**, Act IV,
scene 7)*, 1793
Oil on canvas
Courtesy of the Fogg
Art Museum, Harvard
University Art Museums,
Loan from Margaret
and Henry Erbe
Photographic Services
© President and Fellows
of Harvard College

Figure 13
After drawing by **JEAN
BAPTISTE BERTRAND**
(called **JAMES**)
Ophélie [Ophelia], 1884
Process print of drawing
after painting of 1884
Illustrated in *L'Artiste*,
June 1884
Fine Arts Library,
Harvard University
Courtesy of the
Fine Arts Library,
Harvard College Library

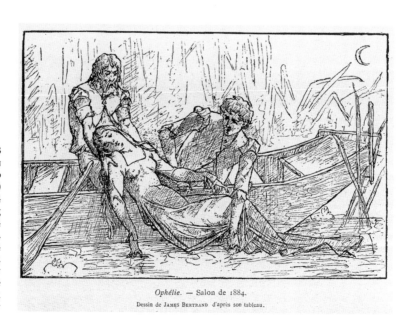

Ophélie. — Salon de 1884.

Dessin de JAMES BERTRAND d'après son tableau.

Théâtre Anglais à Paris.

I cannot chuse but weep, to think,
they should lay him in the cold ground.

M.elle SMITHSON, Rôle d'Offélia dans Hamlet.

Figure 14
Auguste de Valmont
*Mlle Smithson, Rôle d'Offélia
dans **Hamlet** (Théâtre Anglais
à Paris)[Harriet Smithson as
Ophelia in **Hamlet**]*, 1827
Two-toned lithograph,
hand colored
By Permission of the Folger
Shakespeare Library

Figure 15
**Achille Jacques
Jean-Marie Devéria**
After drawing by
Louis Boulanger
***Hamlet**, Acte IV,
Scene 5*, 1827
Lithograph,
hand colored
By Permission
of the Folger
Shakespeare Library

correlative for Hamlet's own."[25] In 1870, possibly with the added stimulus of Millais's painting, the Shakespearean heroine inspired the poem *Ophélie* by Arthur Rimbaud. Not quite sixteen years of age, the young poet recognized in the tragic Ophelia an expression of his own "youthful [and frustrated] desire to communicate the exaltation of his awakening senses and thoughts and [his desire] to celebrate the feeling of a mysterious and transcendent harmony with nature."[26]

> Where the stars sleep in the calm black stream,
> Like some great lily, pale Ophelia floats,
> Slowly floats, wound in her veils like a dream.
> — Half heard in the woods, halloos from distant
> throats.
>
> A thousand years has sad Ophelia gone
> Glimmering on the water, a phantom fair;
> A thousand years her soft distracted song
> Has waked the answering evening air. . .[27]

In the twentieth century, this specific chain of references to Ophelia, from Shakespeare to Millais to Rimbaud, culminates in the 1929 collage still life, *Homage to Rimbaud or Ophelia* by the Bauhaus photographer Walter Peterhans (fig. 16).

Ophelia appears in four of the lithographs in Delacroix's *Hamlet* series (figs. 17–20), the most famous of which is the *Death of Ophelia* of 1843 (fig. 20), and three paintings of the same theme done in 1838, 1844, and 1853, all closely related to the lithograph.[28] One final work, entitled *Ophélie* (fig. 21), is an undated graphite and wash drawing that may or may not originally have been conceived as a representation of Ophelia. The title may have been added when the drawing, a freely washed sketch without any distinguishing Ophelia traits, was selected for use as the sole illustration to *Hamlet* in an undated, extra-illustrated edition of works by Shakespeare published in France, possibly in the early 1860s.[29]

In contrast to the Millais work, Delacroix's treatment of the theme in his *Death of Ophelia* is more overtly sensual and dramatic. The bare-breasted Ophelia is an active participant in the drama. She is captured in the act of falling, her hand clutching the branch of a willow tree. She struggles in vain against the forces of nature. Here, Ophelia becomes "a symbol both of wounded, self-absorbed sexuality and of the destruction of innocence by an indifferent world."[30] In Millais's painting, Ophelia does not resist the forces that act on her. Punctuating the "glassy stream," encased in an exquisite rendering of brightly colored plants, flowers, and other vegetation, her acquiescent, supine body drifts to its "muddy death." Her beautiful face has a

calm, lost gaze, and her lips are slightly parted to emit the sounds of her mad song; her hands extend upward and outward with open palms, a gesture of saint-like submission to death. "In the Shakespearean polarity of nature and civilization," Hana Scolnicov observes, "Ophelia has escaped from the confinement of the male-dominated castle and court to the personal freedom traditionally granted to women by madness and nature."[31]

Figure 16
WALTER PETERHANS
Hommage à Rimbaud ou Ophelia
[Homage to Rimbaud or Ophelia], 1929 (printed 1977)
Gelatin silver print
The Saint Louis Art Museum
Gift of Sander Gallery, Inc.

Millais's painting was executed in two phases. Adhering to the Pre-Raphaelite credo of truth to nature, he did the background outdoors on the banks of the Hogsmill River in Surrey in the summer and fall of 1851. The close attention he gave to rendering each and every plant and flower was perceived by some critics as excessive — an inappropriate and incongruous juxtaposition of nature's richness and the tragic end of a human life. Other criticism focused on what was perceived to be a lack of realism in the position of the body and the stillness of the water around it. As Lisa Nicoletti argues, these critics were uncomfortable with the quality of timelessness in the picture, its lack of closure, which left Ophelia suspended forever between life and death.[32]

Figure 17
EUGÈNE DELACROIX
*Hamlet et Ophélie
(Act. III. Sc. 1) [Hamlet
and Ophelia]*, 1834–1843
Lithograph
By Permission of the
Folger Shakespeare Library

Figure 18
EUGÈNE DELACROIX
*Hamlet fait jouer aux
comédiens la scène de
l'empoisonnement de
son père (Act. III. Sc. 2)
[Hamlet Has the Actors
Play the Scene of his Father's
Poisoning]*, 1835
Lithograph
By Permission of the
Folger Shakespeare Library

Figure 19
EUGÈNE DELACROIX
*Le Chant d'Ophélie (Act. IV.
Sc. 5)[Ophelia's Song]*, 1834
Lithograph
By Permission of the
Folger Shakespeare Library

..........Ses vêtements appesantis et trempés d'eau ont entraîné la pauvre malheureuse.

Figure 20
Eugène Delacroix
Mort d'Ophélie (Act. IV. Sc. 7)
[Death of Ophelia], 1843
Lithograph
By Permission of the
Folger Shakespeare Library

Figure 21
Eugène Delacroix
Hamlet (Ophélie), n.d.
Graphite with brown
and black wash
By Permission of the
Folger Shakespeare Library

"For Millais's contemporaries, Ophelia wasn't quite dead enough."[33] Moreover, the picture did not adhere to the Victorian moral understanding of female suicide. Self-destruction was linked to the life of the fallen woman; it was frequently represented in Victorian art and literature and portrayed as a redemptive act.

Millais added the figure of Ophelia in the studio in the early months of 1852. The model was Elizabeth Siddal (1829–62), the quintessential Pre-Raphaelite muse, beautiful and frail, who, before her premature death in 1862 from a drug overdose, had become an artist, poet, and the wife of Dante Gabriel Rossetti. Dressed in an embroidered gown, she posed in a tin bathtub filled with water warmed by small lamps beneath it. On one occasion, the lamps went out and the water turned cold. Rather than interrupt the artist, she remained in the chilly water and caught a cold severe enough to require the attention of a doctor. This legendary incident of Lizzie in the bathtub is almost as well known as the work itself.

Siddal's story and Ophelia's well-known madness inform Mary Ellen Mark's 1976 documentary photograph *Laurie in the Ward 81 Tub, Oregon State Hospital* (fig. 22). There is a metaphorical association between Millais's painting of Ophelia's watery death and Leeanne Schmidt's untitled 1997 photograph (fig. 23) of a woman whose face and flowing hair are obscured by the turbulent waters engulfing her body. Both images are inscribed in the tradition in myth, art, and literature that links woman with water/nature, the feminine with fluidity, and — following a psychoanalytic model — the identification of woman with death.

The association of Ophelia with nature, with her allegorical reabsorption through death into her natural element, is conveyed in Edward Steichen's 1936 photograph *Lillian Gish as Ophelia* (frontispiece, fig. 24). The photograph was taken at the edge of a pond on Steichen's Connecticut farm when the actress was playing the role at the Empire Theatre. Steichen recounted that he and Gish "had talked about the moment, described in *Hamlet*, when Ophelia 'fell into the weeping brook and drowned.'. . . From the moment she stepped to the edge of the pond and grasped the trailing branch of the willow tree, she was no longer Lillian Gish. She had become Ophelia. . ."[34] Gish, as Ophelia, grasps the branches of the willow tree, and in the rapture of her madness her body is assimilated into nature.

Victor Burgin makes direct use of Millais's *Ophelia* in his large scale, multi-panel, and photo-text work, *The Bridge* (figs. 25, 26).[35] In this work of 1984, the artist explores metaphorical constructions of femininity in relation to the sexual politics of representation and Freudian and neo-Freudian concepts of male desire. *The Bridge* is based both on Millais's painting of *Ophelia* and on the drowning scene from *Vertigo,* Alfred Hitchcock's 1958 film (fig. 27). Influenced by the semiotics of Barthes, Burgin sets into motion a domino effect of associations, memories, ideas, fantasies, and myriad layers of meaning through a conflation of text and images.[36] Ophelia becomes the suicidal, enigmatic Madeleine (Kim Novak), floating in the water under the Golden Gate Bridge. However, in the Hitchcock masterpiece, Madeleine will soon be rescued by Scottie (James Stewart), the obsessive detective under whose watchful eye she becomes an object of desire. Burgin provides an explanation of the symbolic elements and meaning of the work in an introductory panel. He identifies Millais's *Ophelia* as one of many "watery images of women" in the history of representation. He also identifies the "over-arching (over-*bearing*) patriarchal principle [which] readily finds figuration in the image of the bridge. It is by way of such metaphorical tableaux–*allegories*–that the social order is imprinted in the unconscious. In the way that we repeat or recast such tableaux, therefore, there is always more at issue than 'mere metaphor.'"[37]

Burgin's carefully crafted union of Millais's painting and the drowning scene from *Vertigo* uncovers many fields of association, not the least of which are those that already exist between Hitchcock, Shakespeare's *Hamlet,* and Millais's *Ophelia*. As James Vest has observed, many of Hitchcock's films rely on the leitmotif of "a potentially fatal plunge," on the linkage of "water with mutability and death," and on the use of the theme — influenced by literary, artistic, or historical models — of a beautiful girl finding death in a watery grave.[38] The archetype is famously portrayed in *Vertigo*.

Often linked with the traditions of Symbolism and Surrealism, the films of Alfred Hitchcock reflect a vast knowledge of the history of art, and many sources can be identified in his works.[39] Hitchcock also had a lifelong interest in Shakespeare, particularly *Hamlet*, which from his earliest professional years he had planned to direct in a screen version but never did. Hitchcock's double indebtedness to Shakespeare and Millais is most evident in *Vertigo* in the character of Madeleine/Judy, and in the scene of her drowning. Hitchcock borrows many of Millais's compositional and iconographic details: the recumbent form of the drowning figure with extended arms, the voluminous skirt,

Figure 22
Mary Ellen Mark
Laurie in the Ward 81 Tub, Oregon State Hospital, 1976
Gelatin silver print
Mead Art Museum
Purchase with Richard Templeton (Class of 1931) Photography Fund
2000.444
Photo: Stephen Petegorsky

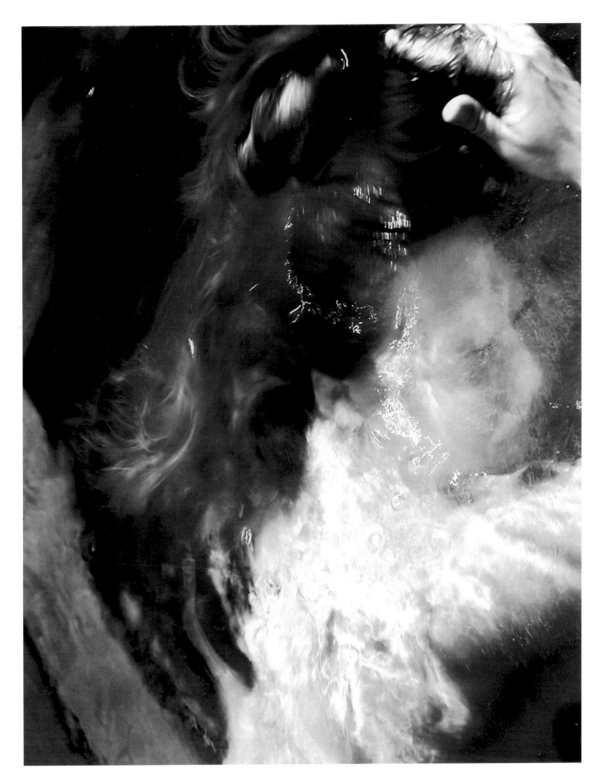

Figure 23
LEEANNE SCHMIDT
Untitled, 1997
Toned gelatin silver print
Mead Art Museum
Purchase with Wise Fund for Fine Arts
2001.571
©Leeanne Schmidt
Photo: Stephen Petegorsky

Figure 25
VICTOR BURGIN
The Bridge, 1984 (detail)
Black and white photo and text construction
With Permission of the artist
Photo: Frank Ward

and flowers floating on the water are the most obvious references. Vest discusses these and identifies still other nineteenth-century depictions of Ophelia to which Hitchcock made references in this scene, including Delacroix's *Death of Ophelia* (fig. 20) from the *Hamlet* lithograph series and Auguste de Valmont's 1827 colored lithograph *Harriet Smithson as Ophelia* (fig. 14), showing Smithson's signature flowing veil, a prop symbolizing Ophelia's madness, echoed in Madeleine's scarf.[40] Several of the same iconographic elements — reclining body in ecstatic position with raised arms and hands, lost gaze, flowers — reappear in Burgin's enigmatic, unattainable Ophelia/Madeleine lying on a flower-covered bed under the Golden Gate Bridge (fig. 26).

A black-and-white reproduction of Millais's famous painting of *Ophelia* made on a photocopy machine with ordinary white copy paper is the departure point for Spanish artist Eugènia Balcells's 1979 artist's book entitled *"OPHELIA" (variacions sobre una imatge [variations on an image]* (figs. 28, 29). The book consists of close to forty images, all of which are in some form or another a repetition of the black-and-white photocopy of Millais's famous painting. The artist demystifies and recontextualizes the image by using ordinary, readymade technical materials and by repeating the image over and over again. In this way, Balcells rebukes the high art status of Millais's painting, removes its aura, and resituates the image in the realm of the ordinary in order to demonstrate the way female sexual identity is constructed in contemporary society through representation. Balcells deconstructs the work through a series of manipulations of the photocopied image, revealing its many personal, popular, and symbolic meanings. For example, in one sequence she subjects the image of Millais's painting to a series of reductions and multiplications until the form of the body of Ophelia is totally broken down and absorbed into a field of broken lines or reduced out of sight on the page. Images overlaid on the photocopied Millais allow Balcells to juxtapose meanings — the high school graduation picture of a girl (presumably the artist); a prayer card with an image of the Virgin; an erotic female nude with raised arms (fig. 29); a woman skier,

Figure 26
VICTOR BURGIN
The Bridge, 1984 (detail)
Black and white photo and text construction
With Permission of the artist
Photo: Frank Ward

Figure 27
Kim Novak in **Vertigo**, 1958
Frame enlargement
Vertigo, Alfred Hitchcock, Director/Producer, 1958
Paris, Cinémathèque française collection
© 1958 Universal City Studios, Inc.
Courtesy of Universal Studios Licensing, Inc.

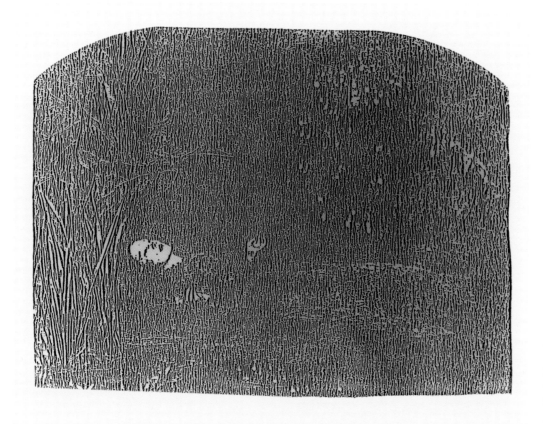

Figure 28
EUGÈNIA BALCELLS
Page from *"OPHELIA"*
(variacions sobre una imatge
[variations on an image], 1979
Barcelona
Artist's book
The Museum of Modern Art
Library, New York
© 2001 Artists Rights Society
(ARS), New York/VEGAP,
Madrid

Figure 29
EUGÈNIA BALCELLS
Page from *"OPHELIA"*
(variacions sobre una imatge
[variations on an image], 1979
Barcelona
Artist's book
The Museum of Modern Art
Library, New York
© 2001 Artists Rights Society
(ARS), New York/VEGAP,
Madrid

strong and athletic, clipped from a woman's magazine.

The most recent incarnation of Millais's *Ophelia* is an untitled work (fig. 30) by the American photographer Gregory Crewdson. Part of the artist's ongoing *Twilight* series (begun 1998), *Untitled (Ophelia)*, 2000–2001, is an elaborately staged, oversized photograph (48 x 60 inches), the making of which was recently featured in *The New York Times Magazine*.[41]   In subject, form, and content, it recalls the painting by Millais. Crewdson's romanticized recreation is set in the domestic realm of modern American suburbia. The body of a woman, dressed in signature white, is suspended in the waters of a flooded living room. The artist describes the scenario as follows:

> I had an image in my mind of this suburban room filled with water. The idea of a floating woman sort of finalized it for me. As I conceived of it, this is a woman who has been living in this house her entire life and who has led up to this point, an everyday existence. She comes down the stairs, and her living room is

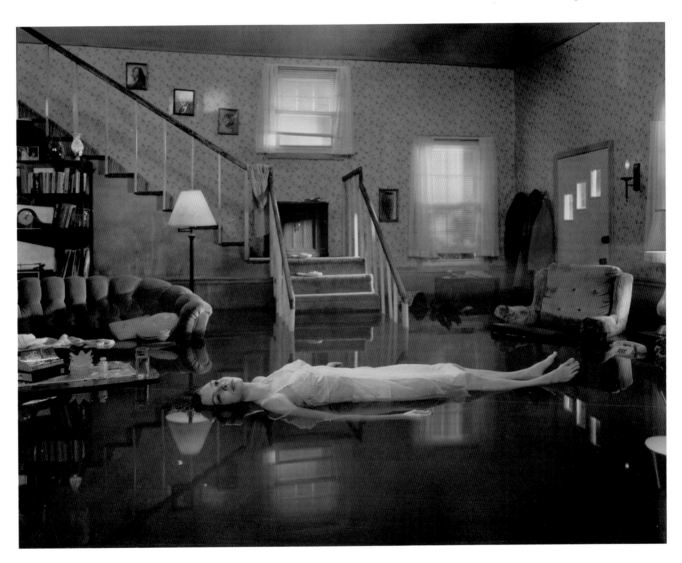

Figure 30
GREGORY CREWDSON
Untitled (Ophelia), 2000–2001
Digital C-print
Edition of 10 with 3 artist's proofs
Courtesy of the artist and
Luhring Augustine, New York

> flooded. She just accepts the situation and submerges herself in the water. That's why the slippers are on the stairs and her robe is on the banister. I see this as a cathartic event, something both beautiful and sad."[42]

Crewdson's photograph displays the sharply focused realism Millais considered so vital in the conception of his work, and it was achieved through a comparable process of staging in order to obtain the accuracy of detail and the desired effect. Just as Millais chose Elizabeth Siddal with great care, Crewdson chose "someone who could really inhabit the character."[43] Siddal's chilly experience in the bathtub reverberates in Crewdson's own recounting of the intense and anxiety-filled shooting of the final version of the photograph. It was a stressful ordeal, and his model, like Siddal, was exposed to physical adversity — the water was freezing! But, Crewdson tells us, never mentioning her name, "the model was. . . determined," and the desired image was successfully achieved.[44]

Overlaid with meaning, the complex, detailed photograph displays the same objectification of the female and the specter of sexuality found in Millais's painting. Evocation of the earlier work, which is also voyeuristic, heightens the richness of Crewdson's image. The presence of Alfred Hitchcock, whose masterpiece *Vertigo* is Crewdson's favorite film, is also felt.[45] As with Hitchcock, the bouquet of the mundane is the mysterious, and there are tensions between the two. Crewdson projects personal meaning on to the "familiar tropes" of suburbia, which, according to the artist, then serve as "surrogates or metaphors for psychological anxiety, fear, or desire."[46] In the making of all of his pictures, Crewdson seeks that which Millais has captured in his *Ophelia*, ". . . that moment of transcendence or transportation, where one is transported to another place, into a perfect still world."[47]

The theme of Ophelia has been particularly compelling for women and girls. Not surprisingly, then, many women artists have treated the subject or have created images alluding to Ophelia. Among those included in the exhibition are artists from the nineteenth century to the present: Julia Margaret Cameron, Anna Lea Merritt, Marie Bashkirtseff, Gwen John, Jean Erdman, Mary Ellen Mark, Eugènia Balcells, Leeanne Schmidt, Louise Bourgeois, and Linda Stark (figs. 10, 22, 23, 28, 29, 32, 33, 35-37, 39, 57).

One of the earliest depictions of Ophelia is by a woman — the little-known, eighteenth-century British artist Mary Hoare (active 1761–1781). Her watercolor and graphite drawing *Ophelia's Death: Hamlet* (fig. 31) is one of a series of seventeen scenes from Shakespeare executed by the artist around 1781. These works, all in the collection of the Yale Center for British Art, constitute almost her entire known output.[48] Hoare's rendering of Ophelia, stretching to hang a garland of flowers on a willow, establishes one of the standard presentations of Ophelia's death more than a decade in advance of the very similar treatment in Westall's influential painting of 1793 (fig. 12).

Ophelia is one of the literary heroines treated by the nineteenth-century British photographer, Julia Margaret Cameron. Her interest in the representation of intangible qualities would have attracted her to the challenge of visualizing Ophelia's madness. Ophelia is represented in three of Cameron's photographs. Two, dating from 1867, are identified as Ophelia by title (figs. 32, 33). Both show the same model, Mary Pinnock, draped in a heavy cloak much like Hugh Diamond's photographic portrait of his Ophelia-like mental patient (fig. 8). Other

Figure 31
Mary Hoare
Ophelia's Death: Hamlet, c. 1781
Watercolor and graphite with some bodycolor
Yale Center for British Art, Paul Mellon Collection

distinguishing Ophelia traits are the long, flowing hair and the presence of flowers in each work, although in neither case is there a strong reliance on props to identify the character. Rather, it is the expression captured in the faces of these women that marks these works. In *Ophelia Study No. 2* (fig. 32), the woman has a distant, trance-like gaze, an effect enhanced by the

Ophelia

Figure 32 (top left)
JULIA MARGARET CAMERON
Ophelia Study No. 2, 1867
Albumen print
Courtesy George Eastman
House

Figure 33 (top right)
JULIA MARGARET CAMERON
Ophelia, 1867
Albumen print
Gernsheim Collection
Harry Ransom Humanities
Research Center
The University of Texas
at Austin

Figure 34
JULIA MARGARET CAMERON
Untitled (Ophelia), 1870/75
Carbon print
The J. Paul Getty Museum,
Los Angeles
© The J. Paul Getty Museum

Figure 35
CLAUDE FAIVRE
After drawing by **MARIE BASHKIRTSEFF**
Ophélie, 1877–1884
Etching
From *L'Artiste*, Jan. 1887
By Permission of the Folger Shakespeare Library, Washington, D.C.

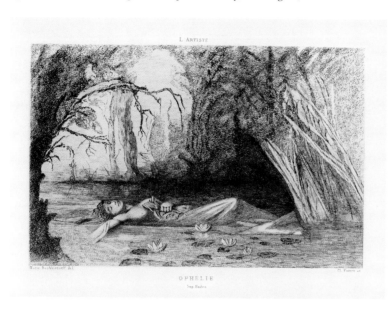

Figure 36
MYRON TANNENBAUM
Jean Erdman Dancing **Ophelia**, 1946
Silver gelatin print
Courtesy of Nancy Allison

intentional blurring of the image. In *Ophelia* (fig. 33), Cameron captures an anxious, almost fearful expression of madness. Cameron's third treatment of the subject is an *Untitled (Ophelia)* (fig. 34), although, of the three works, it is the one most easily recognized as a representation of Ophelia because of its overstated, theatrical effect. Julia Margaret Cameron was a personal friend of the actress Ellen Terry, whom she photographed several times; Terry's husband, the artist George Frederic Watts, painted Terry as Ophelia for the first time in 1864, before she played the part.

Working in Paris from 1877 to 1884, the Russian painter Marie Bashkirtseff executed an image of the dead Ophelia peacefully floating along the surface of the water, an eerie memorial to her own premature death from consumption in 1884 at age 26 (fig. 35). Bashkirtseff's autobiographical representation contributed to the formation of a romanticized cult that developed around the artist soon after her death. She was recognized as one of the most celebrated women artists of her day, but her posthumous fame was based more on the tragedy of her early death and her role as a diarist than on her artistic legacy. Excerpts from her journals, including outpourings about the difficulties a woman artist encountered in the male-dominated Parisian art world, were first published in 1887 in the French periodical *L'Artiste*.[49] Featured among the few illustrations accompanying the texts was an etching after Bashkirtseff's *Ophélie*, an atypical example of her work. It reinforced the identification of Bashkirtseff with Ophelia, now with an emphasis on her physical weakness as symbol of her purity. In the last quarter of the nineteenth century, Bashkirtseff was identified as the living prototype for the *"femme fragile,"* an idealized conception of femininity defined by delicacy, tubercular weakness, and frailty, explored by Bram Dijkstra as "a cult of invalidism," and celebrated in the works of a host of turn-of-the-century writers and artists.[50]

Movement is the vehicle for expressing the emotional torment of madness in the 1946 dance *Ophelia* (fig. 36) by Jean Erdman. Born in Honolulu in 1916, this American modern dancer and choreographer studied with and then performed as a soloist under Martha Graham in the early 1940s. She started her own dance group in 1944, collaborating on occasion with the dancer Merce Cunningham and the composer John

Figure 37
Louise Bourgeois
Hamlet and Ophelia, 1996–97, published 1997
Five color lithograph
Mead Art Museum
Purchase with William W. Collins (Class of 1953) Print Fund
2001.570
Photo: Stephen Petegorsky

Cage. Influenced by Jungian psychology, Erdman's dance explores the experience of the fragile Ophelia, "for whom the life experience is so terrifying that it cannot be integrated into the psyche and it leads instead to total dismemberment."[51] Ophelia's mental anguish is captured in the intensity of the rhythms of Cage's music. The flowing white costume was designed by Xenia Cage and Jean Erdman; it features bright red nerve endings painted along the inside of the arms and torso. The title *Ophelia* was proposed by Erdman's husband, the celebrated author and scholar of myth, Joseph Campbell.

Ophelia's tragic narrative is given a fairy-tale ending in the Mead's newly acquired five-color lithograph, *Hamlet and Ophelia*, 1996-97, by Louise Bourgeois (fig. 37). In the coital embrace of her lover, Ophelia, with long flowing hair and high-heeled shoes, is submerged, not in the muddy waters of a brook, but in a sea of undulating bright blue water. Vivid colors and repeating lines in wavy rhythmic motion give energy to the composition and definition to the forms. But all is not well in Denmark: Hamlet is above the water line, Ophelia beneath. Is she the "self-sacrificial corpse," the beautiful "dead woman as object of erotic desire"?[52] Bourgeois's *Hamlet and Ophelia* is one of a series of prints of the 1990s with themes of love, sex, and death. As noted by Carol Smith, it is closely related to *Bed #2 (Red Bed)*, 1997 which shows another embracing couple, here under a literal blanket of love — one end transformed into a pair of giant lips.[53] That Bourgeois should be attracted to the theme of Ophelia is not surprising; in the fifty-year span of her artistic career, she has devoted herself to the representation, often highly personal, of female identity or the role of woman as mother, daughter, sister, or lover. One of several prints made by Bourgeois to benefit charitable causes or institutions, *Hamlet and Ophelia* was issued for the Brooklyn Academy of Music. In the 1997 season of its Next Wave Festival, the Brooklyn Academy of Music featured Robert Lapage's one-man version of *Hamlet, Elsinore*. In this high-tech spectacle, Peter Darling delivers Gertrude's speech wearing a white gilded dress (fig. 38). At the end of the speech, a stunning transformation is set in motion as the suicide of Ophelia is enacted. As described by Richard Knowles:

> … the dress broke away from the actor like the encrustation from a pupa, and Ophelia emerged embryonic in a flimsy white undergown partially open at the chest to reveal the male body beneath, evoking an effective androgyny that was reinforced by the

falsetto singing of a medley . . . of Ophelia's songs. . . . At this point the actor-as-Ophelia crossed to center stage . . . and lay down on a vast blue cloth, his/her arms crossed, as the stage mechanism slowly rose — all but a rectangular coffin-shaped opening at its center, into which the body seemed to sink, engulfed by the watery drapery that slid into the grave-like opening to enshroud her. As the machinery lifted, however, the same actor, as Hamlet, emerged from beneath it completing a breathtaking . . . series of metamorphoses.[54]

In Ophelia iconography water is associated with tragic content. In Linda Stark's *Ophelia Forever* (fig. 39),

Figure 38
CLAUDEL HUOT
Peter Darling as Ophelia in Robert Lapage's
Hamlet, Elsinore, *1997*
Silver gelatin print, 1997
Courtesy Ex Machina, Quebec City

however, it achieves a celebratory status. Erect nipples and effervescent bubbles are symbols of Ophelia's ecstasy in this pop-surrealist work. Humorous and emblematic, this 1999 oil on canvas teeters deceptively on the brink of cliché, yet beneath its surface are Stark's personal, childhood memories of the ecstasy of a near-death drowning experience. In this work, the artist declares the regenerative power of the female spirit. "With nipple eyes wrapped in the black bra of an infinity symbol, the painting stares back at the viewer, as a goddess looking through eyeglasses."[55]

Historically approached and contextualized, images of Ophelia reflect the norms and stereotypes of the

Figure 39
LINDA STARK
Ophelia Forever, 1999
Oil on canvas on panel
Courtesy of the Artist and Angles Gallery
Santa Monica, CA
Private Collection, Glendale, CA

culture in which they are produced and received. They can be shown to participate, often subtly, in the process of forming, perpetuating, transgressing, and destroying existing norms and stereotypes. The archetype, which Shakespeare captured so memorably in his Ophelia, never seems to struggle for relevance, so willingly does it adapt to changes of time, place, and ideology. As the expanding body of art and literature will attest, Ophelia is a subject of endless revision and variation. Born of Shakespeare, she lives in the ideological present, transformed and reinvented in response to the cultural needs of each successive society which adopts her as its own. ❧

Notes

[1] References to *Hamlet* are from The Arden Shakespeare, edited by Harold Jenkins (London: Methuen, 1982).

[2] This is noted with other examples by Kaara Peterson, "Framing Ophelia: Representation and the Pictorial Tradition," *Mosaic*, 31, no. 3 (September 1998): 19–20, and Elaine Showalter, "Representing Ophelia: Women, Madness, and the Responsibilities of Feminist Criticism," *Shakespeare and the Question of Theory*, ed. Patricia Parker and Geoffrey Hartman (New York: Methuen, 1985): 78. Showalter's essay has become a standard source for any study of the representation of Ophelia.

[3] Mary Pipher, *Reviving Ophelia: Saving the Selves of Adolescent Girls* (New York: Ballantine Books, 1994); Sara Shandler, *Ophelia Speaks: Adolescent Girls Write about Their Search for Self* (New York: Harper Collins, 1999); Nina Shandler, *Ophelia's Mom: Women Speak Out about Loving and Letting Go of Their Adolescent Daughters* (New York: Crown Publishers, 2001).

[4] www.ehow.com.

[5] Roland Barthes, *Image, Music, Text*, ed. and trans. Stephen Heath (New York: The Noonday Press, 1977) 47, 148.

[6] Most recent studies include: Peterson, cited above, an excellent interdisciplinary essay combining literary and art historical methodologies; Lisa Nicoletti, "Resuscitating Ophelia: Images of Suicide and Suicidal Insanity in Nineteenth-Century England," Ph.D. diss., University of Wisconsin-Madison, 1999; Kimberly Rhodes, "Performing Roles: Images of Ophelia in Britain, 1740–1910," Ph.D. diss., Columbia University, 1999. The latter is a very thorough study of the subject in nineteenth-century Britain, although exception is taken to her claim [p.4] that images of Ophelia "virtually disappeared" in the twentieth century. Several essays in *Shakespeare Yearbook*, 11, 2000, published as Holger

Klein and James L. Harner, eds., *Shakespeare and the Visual Arts* (Lewiston, Queenston, Lampeter: The Edwin Mellen Press, 2000) are on the theme of Ophelia, others are on *Hamlet* with a major Ophelia focus. Of the former, these include: Martha Tuck Rozett, "Drowning Ophelias and Other Images of Death in Shakespeare's Plays," 182–196; B. R. Siegfried, "Ethics, Interpretation, and Shakespeare's Ophelia: The Re-emergence of Visual Phronesis in the Works of Maclise, Rossetti, Préault, and Abbey," 197–226; Hanna Scolnicov, "Intertextuality and Realism in Three Versions of *Hamlet*: The Willow Speech and the Aesthetics of Cinema," 227–237; R. Scott Fraser, "On Ophelia," 238–259; Alan R. Young, "*Hamlet* and Nineteenth-Century Photography," 260–307. Also, the Website maintained by Harry Rusche, *Shakespeare Illustrated*, Emory University, http://www.emory.edu/ENGLISH/classes/Shakespeare_ Illustrated/Shakespeare.html

[7] Richard D. Altick, *Paintings from Books: Art and Literature in Britain, 1760–1900* (Columbus: Ohio State University Press, 1985) 299.

[8] From his 1765 edition of the plays of Shakespeare, as quoted in John Jump, ed., *Shakespeare: Hamlet, A Casebook* (London: Macmillan, 1968) 24.

[9] The painting is in the Cincinnati Art Museum, Cincinnati, Ohio.

[10] Mary Floyd-Wilson, "Ophelia and Femininity in the Eighteenth Century: 'Dangerous conjectures in ill-breeding minds,'" *Women's Studies*, 21 (1992): 407.

[11] The summary presented here is drawn primarily from Showalter, 77–94. Also, see Elaine Showalter, *The Female Malady: Women, Madness and English Culture, 1830–1980* (New York: Pantheon Books, 1985).

[12] The essays were published in installments in 1858 in the *Medical Times and Gazette*. See Sander L. Gilman, ed. *The Face of Madness, Hugh Diamond and the Origin of Psychiatric Photography* (New York: Brunner/Mazel, 1976) 15, n. 16.

[13] John Conolly, *A Study of Hamlet* (London: Edward Moxon & Co, 1863) 168.

[14] Conolly 177–78.

[15] Bucknill, as quoted in Showalter 86.

[16] Conolly 178.

[17] Quoted in Young, 2000, 287, n. 13.

[18] Showalter 86. The quote is from Ellen Terry, *The Story of My Life* (London: Hutchinson & Co., 1908) 154.

[19] Galina Gorokhoff, ed., *Love Locked Out: The Memoirs of Anna Lea Merritt with A Checklist of Her Works* (Boston: Museum of Fine Arts, 1981) 130.

[20] Anna Lea Merritt, in Gorokhoff 130. My emphasis.

[21] Anna Lea Merritt, in Gorokhoff 130.

[22] The work was one of 22 paintings by Westall commissioned by Alderman John Boydell for exhibition at the "Shakespeare Gallery." It was engraved by James Parker and published by John and Josiah Boydell in George Steevens's 1802 edition of *The Dramatic Works of Shakespeare*.

[23] Nina Auerbach, *Romantic Imprisonment: Women and Other Glorified Outcasts* (New York: Columbia University Press, 1986) 282.

[24] Auerbach 282.

[25] James M. Vest, *The French Face of Ophelia from Belleforest to Baudelaire* (Lanham, New York, and London: University Press of America, 1989) 179.

[26] Valerie Minogue, "Rimbaud's *Ophelia*," *French Studies: A Quarterly Review*, 43, no. 4 (Oct. 1989): 424.

[27] The poem is in three parts, two of four quatrains, and the third of one. The first two quatrains of the first part are quoted. Arthur Rimbaud, *Complete Works*, trans. Paul Schmidt (New York: HarperPerennial, 2000) 28–30.

[28] The paintings are located in the Neue Pinakothek, Munich (1838); the Oskar Reinhart Collection, Winterthur (1844); and the Louvre (1853).

[29] I would like to thank Erin Blake and Deborah Leslie of the Folger Shakespeare Library for assistance in trying to establish the date of the volume. See catalogue checklist for complete title and other bibliographic information.

[30] Peter Raby, *'Fair Ophelia': A Life of Harriet Smithson Berlioz* (Cambridge: Cambridge University Press, 1982) 182.

[31] Scolnicov 231.

[32] Nicoletti 180.

[33] Nicoletti 180.

[34] Edward Steichen, *A Life in Photography* (Garden City, New York: Doubleday & Co., 1963) n.p.

[35] For illustration of the complete work and discussion, see *Victor Burgin*, essays by Peter Wollen, Francette Pacteau, Norman Bryson, exh. cat., Fundació Antonio Tàpies, Barcelona, 2001, 151–162.

[36] Peter Wollen, "Barthes, Burgin, *Vertigo*," in *Victor Burgin* 19.

[37] Victor Burgin, Introductory text panel from *The Bridge*, reprinted in *Victor Burgin* 151.

[38] James M. Vest, "Reflections of Ophelia (and of Hamlet) in Alfred Hitchcock's *Vertigo*," *Journal of the Midwest Modern Language Association*," 22 (1989): 1, 6.

[39] See Dominique Païni and Guy Cogeval, eds., *Hitchcock and Art: Fatal Coincidences*, exh. cat., Montreal Museum of Fine Arts, Montreal, 2001.

[40] Vest 1, 2.

[41] Nelson Hancock, "The Ultimate Film Still: The Art Photographer Gregory Crewdson Shares Tales from the Set of His Latest Production," *The New York Times Magazine* (March 25, 2001): 50–53.

[42] Hancock 52.

[43] Hancock 52.

[44] Hancock 52.

[45] *Gregory Crewdson: Dream of Life*, exh. cat., Salamanca: Ediciones Universidad de Salamanca, 1999, 27.

[46] *Gregory Crewdson: Dream of Life* 21.

[47] Gregory Crewdson from "Egg Interview with Gregory Crewdson," produced by Maria Patrick, *Egg: the arts show*, WNET/New York, July 26, 2001, www.pbs.org/wnet/egg.

[48] See Geoffrey Ashton, *Shakespeare and British Art*, exh. cat., Yale Center for British Art, New Haven, 1981, 27–30.

[49] Marie Bashkirtseff, "Journal posthume d'une artiste (Fragments)," *L'Artiste*, vol. 1 (jan., fév. 1887); 58–64; 122–131.

[50] Bram Dijkstra, "The Cult of Invalidism; Ophelia and Folly; Dead Ladies and the Fetish of Sleep," Chapter 2 in *Idols of Perversity: Fantasies of Feminine Evil in Fin-de-Siècle Culture* (New York and Oxford: Oxford University Press, 1986) 25–63. Also, see Gudrun Brokoph-Mauch, "Salome and Ophelia: The Representation of Women in Fin-de-Siècle Austrian Literature," *Modern Austrian Literature* 22, nos. 3–4 (1989): 241–255.

[51] Jean Erdman, *Dance and Myth: The World of Jean Erdman, Part 1. The Early Dances*, executive producer, Nancy Allison (New York: Mystic Fire Video, 1995).

[52] See discussion of this theme in nineteenth and early twentieth century art in Dijkstra 42–63.

[53] Carol Smith, *Louise Bourgeois Prints: 1989–1998*, exh. cat., Maier Museum of Art, Randolph-Macon Woman's College, Lynchburg, Virginia, 1999, 17–18.

[54] Richard Paul Knowles, "The Real of It Would Be Awful: Representing the Real Ophelia in Canada," *Theatre Survey*, 39, no. 1 (May 1998): 24.

[55] Linda Stark, e-mail correspondence via Angles Gallery, July 20, 2001.

Ophelia

Figure 40
MARCUS STONE
Ophelia, 1896
Goupilgravure
By Permission of the Folger Shakespeare Library

Sweet Rose of May:
Ophelia through Victorian Eyes

Georgianna Ziegler

Folger Shakespeare Library

phelia was one of the pet dreams of my girlhood — partly, perhaps, from the mystery of her madness." This sentiment might apply to any number of young women who weave their anxieties and dreams through Ophelia Websites today, but in fact it was written by the nineteenth-century actress Helena Faucit Martin, who recalled her fascination with Shakespeare's character many years before she was to perform the role on stage.[1] Martin's youthful reaction to Ophelia is captured by chance in an 1836 women's annual, *Friendship's Offering*, which includes a reproduction of a painting by J. W. Wright called *The Friends*. The painting shows two girls, the taller one with blond hair reading a book, the shorter one with dark hair leaning on her shoulder and looking down at the book. Accompanying the illustration is a poem by Thomas Miller, entitled "Reading Shakespeare." It begins:

> Far in a wood's sad solitary gloom,
> Two maidens sat beneath an aged tree,
> In leafy summer's sweet expanding bloom:
> A brook rolled by in mournful minstrelsy,
> Bordered with sweetest flowers, and mosses
>   curled; —
> There they communed with him whose fame yet
>   fills the world.
>
> And as the stream stole murmuringly along,
> Their kindled fancies with its music rose;
> And their ears caught Ophelia's dying song,
> Down the deep waters sinking to a close;
> A pensive willow, drooping from the land,
> Lower appeared to bend, grasped by her pale thin
>   hand.[2]

The romantic melancholy and sadness evoked by the death of this young girl captured the fancy of Victorians. Martin followed Mary Cowden Clarke in imagining a pre-Shakespearean girlhood for Ophelia. They saw her as the only daughter of an elderly father, whose mother had died when she was born, and who lacked the close friendship of another young woman from her own social status. In order to explain how such an innocent girl would know the bawdy songs she sings during her madness, they imagined her growing up in the care of a peasant nurse and her family. Alongside this fleshing-out of the Shakespearean character, Victorians also made her more than human in their idealization of her. They saw in her the quintessential innocence and purity of young womanhood on the verge of sexual awakening, but unable to reach maturity because of her inability to live under the terms of the cold, hard world.[3]

A seminal work in the process of idealization was Anna Jameson's *Characteristics of Women, Moral, Poetical, and Historical*, first published in London in 1832 then numerous times throughout the century. Jameson uses Shakespeare's heroines as examples of different types of female behavior. For her, Ophelia is one in whom "the feminine character appears resolved into its very elementary principles — as modesty, grace, tenderness. . . . *Without* these, a woman is no woman . . ."[4] Jameson continues:

> Shakspeare then has shown us that these elemental feminine qualities . . . when expanded under genial influences, suffice to constitute a perfect and happy human creature: such is Miranda [in *The Tempest*]. When thrown alone amid harsh and adverse destinies, and amid the trammels and corruptions of society, without energy to resist, or will to act, or strength to endure, the end must needs be desolation. Ophelia — poor Ophelia! O far too soft, too good, too fair, to be cast among the briers of this working-day world, and fall and bleed upon the thorns of life.[5]

Jameson compares Ophelia to "a strain of sad sweet music," a snow-flake, and the perfume of a violet, all delicate and beautiful things which perish almost instantly.[6] Later she compares her to a dove caught in a tempest.[7] Ophelia is "more conscious of being loved [by Hamlet] than of loving," but she loves nevertheless and keeps it secret.[8] As Christianity "has taught us to . . . worship . . . the symbols of purity and innocence," so Hamlet in his "soaring, penetrating genius" still reposes "upon the tender virgin innocence of Ophelia."[9] But in the manner of a Greek tragedy, the play sweeps the guilty and the innocent to death, making of Ophelia "a spotless victim offered up to the mysterious and inexorable fates."[10] In the earlier editions of her work that include Jameson's own illustrations, she ends Ophelia's story with a vignette showing the lovely young woman dead, with her long hair splayed out behind her head, her wet robes revealing the sensuous outlines of her body, just pulled from the water. Over her hover the three hooded "mysterious" fates, with a moon in the sky, that signifies Jameson's last line, "But there's a heaven above us!"[11] The three fates I think also incorporate those three feminine virtues exemplified by Ophelia: modesty, grace, and tenderness.

Jameson's use of terms such as *dove, briers, thorns, worship, virgin innocence,* and *victim* place Ophelia within a definite religious setting that is adopted by other writers and artists during the century. In 1837, Charles Heath produced the first of two popular sets of engravings illustrating Shakespeare's heroines; these soon replaced Jameson's own pictures in later editions of her *Characteristics* and also in editions of Mary Cowden Clarke's *The Girlhood of Shakespeare's Heroines*. The earlier 1836 Ophelia by John Bostock (fig. 41) looks more holy and pure than mad, as she stands dressed in

Figure 41
W. Joseph Edwards
After a drawing of 1836 by John Bostock
Ophelia (**Hamlet**. *Act IV, Scene 5*), after 1836
Engraving
By Permission of the Folger Shakespeare Library

a white robe, her hands clasped holding flowers at her breast, with more flowers and straw garlanding the dark hair that flows over her shoulders. The straw garland here and in some other pictures (see especially Mortimer's 1775 drawing *Ophelia* (fig. 7) and Delacroix's 1834 lithograph *Ophelia's Song* [fig. 19]), while signifying madness (as in images of King Lear), also recalls Christ's crown of thorns.

Figure 42
SAMUEL JAMES BOUVERIE HAYDON
With the collaboration of FRANCIS SEYMOUR HADEN
After pen and ink drawing of 1858 by DANTE GABRIEL ROSSETTI
Hamlet. Act III, scene 1, Ophelia Returning the Gift to Hamlet, c. 1880
Etching, printed in dark brown ink
By Permission of the Folger Shakespeare Library

HAMLET.

Figure 43
Charles Rolls
After painting by Daniel Maclise
The Play Scene from Hamlet, 1842
Engraving
By Permission of the Folger Shakespeare Library

In the nineteenth century, artists most often chose to represent Ophelia alone just before her watery death, but there are also representations of her in the so-called "Nunnery scene" (Act III, scene 1) (figs. 17, 42); at court during the "Mousetrap scene" (Act III, scene 2) (figs. 2, 3, 18, 43); and distributing flowers, after she is mad (Act IV, scene 5) (figs. 4, 5, 44).[12] The "Nunnery scene," where Ophelia is set up by Claudius and Polonius to test Hamlet's sanity, provoked mixed responses from Victorian critics. On the one hand were those such as Madeleine Leigh-Noel who felt that at this crucial moment, Ophelia failed Hamlet when he needed her: "She closed the door of refuge on his 'betossed soul'."[13] A middle view was taken by Helena Martin who argues that Ophelia agreed to be used as a bait for Hamlet only to find out if her "soul's idol" really *does* love her, after his strange, mad entrance into her chamber. "She will test his affection by offering to return his love-tokens, his gifts and letters — anything to end this torturing suspense."[14] On the other hand there are those who felt that Ophelia could do no wrong. Louis Lewes wrote, "She appears at court like an angel surrounded by an atmosphere of heaven. . . . Her helplessness touches us the more because it springs from her innocence, not from her weakness. Her feelings are strongly developed before she herself is strong enough to bear them."[15] A late nineteenth-century actress, writing about her own performance of Ophelia, noted that "The virginal soul of the fair Ophelia, slipping slowly but irrevocably into the golden ecstasy of first love, is so happy in the strange, exquisite joy of loving ideally, and being so beloved, that practical mundane matters of propriety . . . have not yet entered her mind."[16] The actress believed that Ophelia was hurt when she realized that "the delicious, sacred secret" of Hamlet's love for her was the topic of common conversation; that her idea of love and Hamlet's gifts to her she had enshrined "as most holy sacraments."[17] The religious language here — *sacred, holy sacraments* — only idealizes what we recognize as a girl's first "crush" — the young, unworldly woman falling in love with the jaded "older man." Nevertheless, elements of religion in the play itself have been explored by modern critics.

In particular, they have noted how the staging of the "Nunnery scene" "suggests the iconography of the Annunciation."[18] But while Ophelia, like the Virgin, stands, sits, or kneels with her book of prayers, the Hamlet who suddenly appears to her is no Gabriel, and his first words, "Nymph, in thy orisons / Be all my sins remembered" (Act III, scene 1, 89–90) can be seen to mock the angel's announcement, "Hail Mary, full of grace," a Protestant castigation of the Catholic belief in the Virgin as intercessor.[19] A different, more reverential reading of the scene may be found in the 1858 drawing by Dante Gabriel Rossetti, etched by Samuel James B. Haydon around 1880 (fig. 42).[20] Fascinated by the relationship between Hamlet and Ophelia, Rossetti returned to the subject again and again, depicting the encounter with Hamlet in her chamber, the "Nunnery scene," her first madness, and a scene not in the play, Hamlet kissing her hand by a window.[21] It is the "Nunnery scene," however, that is most charged with religious imagery.

The setting looks like a medieval chapel with heavily-carved high benches. The figure of Hamlet, dressed in a dark monk-like robe, dominates the center of the picture. He kneels on the seat, his outstretched arms suggesting the crucified Christ. His right hand crushes the petals of a white rose from a bush, while his left hand is extended over Ophelia, who turns her head away from him, as she sits in the corner of the bench, an open book in her lap, her right hand extending letters and a necklace to Hamlet. Though her body is turned towards us, the viewer, her glance looks back at him, almost fearfully, as the Virgin sometimes reacts to Gabriel.[22] In an alcove next to Ophelia rests a crucifix, suggesting that she will be the innocent victim of Hamlet's world, as he symbolically crushes her in the white rose. Beneath Hamlet's right arm, two Biblical scenes carved on a chair further suggest the rich levels of religious symbolism with which Rossetti imbues his picture. At the top, the Tree of Knowledge encircled by a crowned serpent is flanked by two angels holding swords, and the inscription: *Eritis sicut deus* [sic] *scientes bonum et malum* [You will be as a god, knowing both good and evil.] Below is carved the story of Uzzah from II Samuel, showing him dying after touching the Ark of the Covenant to keep it from falling. The appropriateness of this rather obscure story from the Old Testament has been explained by one critic as representing the idea that "no good deed goes unpunished," or that it is dangerous "to do anything in God's service without his express word."[23] Ophelia believes she is doing a good deed by obeying her father and trying to find out what is wrong with Hamlet, and the similar gesturing positions of Uzzah's arm and Ophelia's arm have been noted.[24] But I think we can also read the iconography as suggesting that the world of Hamlet's Denmark is our world after the Fall; it is a world that cannot support innocence or well-meaning gestures, but destroys the good — Uzzah, Christ, Ophelia and even Hamlet — as well as itself.

Ophelia next appears at court in the "Mousetrap scene" — Hamlet's staging of a play to "catch" Claudius. One of the most influential depictions of this scene occurs in the great painting by Daniel Maclise, exhibited at the Royal Academy in 1842, and distributed widely through engravings (fig. 43). Dressed in white, her blonde head bowed and hands clasped lightly as though in prayer, Ophelia stands out from the mostly-darkened figures of the rest of the court. She is an oasis of light and calm between a watchful Horatio who stands just behind her, and a frowning Hamlet lounging at her feet, his eyes on Claudius. Her figure illustrates perfectly Lewes's remark that "she appears at court like an angel surrounded by an atmosphere of heaven."[25]

depictions of this scene and of her death. An early nineteenth-century watercolor by Thomas Uwins, engraved as an illustration to Ophelia's mad scene (Act IV, scene 5), shows Ophelia cowed beneath Gertrude, Claudius, and Horatio as though she were a sacrifice; indeed, Claudius's red cloak, hat, and beard make him a devil-like figure.[26] Ophelia herself, dressed in white with flowers before her, kneels in their midst and raises her eyes to heaven. She is, as Lewes described her, "the spotless victim of a pitiless destiny."[27] The anonymous nineteenth-century Actress who left her memoirs, describes her saintly, spiritualized performance of this scene:

> She is in simple white garments and wears a white veil over her head, Madonna-wise, giving one the first impression of a nun, as she appears. . . . She wears, as a rosary, the chain that Hamlet refused to recognise, in the links of which she has stuck purple pansies for beads, and at the end there still hangs his portrait. . . . Gazing with tense sombreness before her, she mechanically lifts her veil over her head, as on her first entrance, murmuring still: 'God 'a' mercy on his soul,' as she fingers the blossoms on her chain-rosary for prayer-beads. But instead of a cross she touches, at the end there, Hamlet's portrait. She lifts it up, gazes on it in silence for an anguished second, then shelters it against her breast, and, raising her eyes to heaven in piteous appeal, adds in a murmur of infinite pathos: 'And on *all* Christian souls, I pray God!' Wrapt in her prayer, she seems to become more and more remote from her surroundings.[28]

Figure 44
FRIEDRICH AUGUST MORITZ RETZSCH
*Ophelia (**Hamlet**, Act IV, Sc. 5)*, 1828
Graphite drawing
By Permission of the Folger Shakespeare Library

When we next see Ophelia, however, her father has been killed, Hamlet is gone, and she has sunk into madness (fig. 44). The notion of her as victim, raised in the "Nunnery scene," is carried through in some of the

Ophelia's flowers themselves received reverential treatment. A set of colored lithographs from designs by Jane E. Giraud in *The Flowers of Shakspeare* printed in 1845 by Day and Haghe, Lithographers to the Queen, present two bouquets of Ophelia's flowers.[29] The first from Act IV, scene 5 includes her speech, "There's rosemary, that's for remembrance," while the second arranges the flowers from the "fantastic garland" at her death, Act IV, scene 7. The "T" of "There's rosemary" is shown as a wooden

Figure 45
Arthur Hughes
Ophelia, 1852
Oil on canvas
© Manchester City Art Galleries

cross entwined with flowers, while a little weeping angel with wings outspread forms the "T" of "There is a willow." Such popular sentimentalizing shows how broadly perceived among the Victorians was the notion of Ophelia's purity, innocence, and victimization.

It was Ophelia's death itself, however — a scene described but not played onstage — that elicited the most pictorial representations. Many artists showed her strewn with flowers, caught in her own thoughts in the moments before her death. Richard Westall's 1793 painting for the Boydell Gallery was one of the first to depict Ophelia garlanding the willow before she slips into the stream beneath (fig. 12). Disseminated widely through engravings, Westall's painting directly influenced many other representations of the scene. In his work, however, the light on her white gown and glowing in the sky just beyond her sheds an otherworldly aura over the sad event. In quite a different style, but even more religiously evocative is the strange Pre-Raphaelite painting of *Ophelia* by Arthur Hughes (1852), now in the City of Manchester Art Galleries (fig. 45). The central figure shows a wispy, young girl, dressed in white and crowned with rushes like those she holds in her arms, her eyes bent down into a murky stream, while all around her is a swampy landscape, evoking Hamlet's cry about the world as an overgrown garden, "Things rank and gross possess it merely." The painting is arch-shaped and set into a gold frame on which is inscribed part of Gertrude's speech describing Ophelia's death: "There is a willow . . . ." The gold frame elicits from the viewer a holy or worshipful attitude toward the central white-garbed figure it contains. This style of framing became popular among the Pre-Raphaelites, who used it for religious and secular works alike, but in this instance it enhances the sense of holiness already suggested by the clear mysterious light that sets off Ophelia's rush/thorn-crowned figure from the blasted landscape.[30]

Other artists used different techniques to enhance Ophelia's "holiness." John Wood's *Ophelia* (fig. 46) shows a young dark-eyed girl, in the tradition of "beauties" portraits (figs. 54, 56), dressed in white and kneeling beside a stream.[31] Her madness appears to have given way to a moment of prayerful calm before death, as she clasps her hands and raises her eyes away from the stream to a light shining from beyond the picture plane. In a painting by Henry LeJeune, Ophelia becomes both subject and object of sacrifice as she hangs her garland on a bough over the water and looks to heaven.[32] Domenico Tojetti's *Ophelia*, painted in 1880,

shows her as a Magdalen figure, dressed in white satin, her hair flowing and eyes raised to heaven, as she sits on the ground with white roses and other flowers strewn before her;[33] and Marcus Stone's *Ophelia* (fig. 40), done in 1896 for the *Graphic Gallery* magazine, shows her also dressed in white and kneeling in earnest prayer, her hands resting on flowers and a white veil, which signifies her aborted marriage to Hamlet, remembered in Gertrude's lines at her funeral, "I hop'd thou shouldst have been my Hamlet's wife: / I thought thy bride-bed to have deck'd, sweet maid" (Act V, scene 1, 237–38). The ubiquitous white gown, veil, and roses are emblematic of her girlhood and purity.[34]

Figure 46
Charles Rolls
After painting of 1831 by **John Wood**
Ophelia, after 1831
Engraving
By Permission of the Folger Shakespeare Library

Though Millais's 1852 painting of Ophelia's death is the most famous rendering of this scene (fig. 11), it does not project as obvious a religious feeling as do some other representations, probably because Millais's focus is on the exact rendering of the physicality of the scene:

plants, water, and the woman's face and hands. In fact, Millais was criticized at the time for his interpretation: "'There is no pathos, no melancholy . . . If she die swan-like with a song, there is no sound or melody, no poetry in this strain.'"[35] Millais's *Ophelia* was given poetic voice by his model for the painting, Elizabeth Siddal. In the bizarre way that life sometimes mirrors art, Lizzie's own relationship with Dante Gabriel Rossetti loosely replicated that of Ophelia and Hamlet: first she was loved by him, then they separated, then feeling sorry for her he married her, but she descended into madness and death. Some have seen her poem, "A Year and a Day," as recalling her lost love through the feelings of Ophelia looking up through the watery grasses:[36]

> I lie among the tall green grass
> That bends above my head
> And covers up my wasted face
> And folds me in its bed
> Tenderly and lovingly
> Like grass above the dead.
>
> A shadow falls along the grass
> And lingers at my feet;
> A new face lies between my hands –
> Dear Christ, if I could weep
> Tears to shut out the summer leaves
> When this new face I greet.
>
> Still it is but the memory
> Of something I have seen
> In the dreamy summer weather
> When the green leaves came between;
> The shadow of my dear love's face –
> So far and strange it seems.[37]

Christ is evoked twice in the poem as an exclamation that is half-prayer, both times associated with the green leaves of death that threaten the returning vision of the lover's face. The experience of lost love and death, told from the woman's point of view, is both mystical and frightening, different from the romantic and beautiful image created by many male artists.[38]

Nineteenth-century male artists in particular seem to have been fascinated with the dead, young, and beautiful female figure, represented in major paintings not only by Ophelia, but by the Arthurian character Elaine, who died for love of Lancelot and was set adrift on a boat; and by the Lady of Shalott from Tennyson's poem, also depicted by Millais, floating downriver to her death.[39] This *Lustmord* was taken to its extreme in the death-mask by Domenico Trentacoste (c. 1894), presumably of a female model made to look like the dead Ophelia.[40] The serene face beneath flower-decked hair is like other period portraits of young women, lying in the peace of death. As Elizabeth Bronfen notes, such "representations of a beautiful woman's dead body" were a way of purifying and distancing "from two moments of insecurity — female sexuality and decay."[41] The problem, explored by Kaara Peterson, is that Ophelia is not a real person but a character in a play, and furthermore, we never actually see her die; her death is reported in a poetic set-piece by Gertrude which is then translated in myriad pictorial forms by artists. These are, to quote Bronfen again, "representations of representations . . . twice removed from their object of reference."[42] Carried to its extreme, Peterson suggests that "the representations of Ophelia might turn out to be even less about her history than they might chronicle the continuing significance of Shakespeare for many cultures . . . ."[43] It might further be argued, that attempts to construct "ethereal" or "holy" Ophelias only replicate the Victorian creation of "Saint Shakespeare," that idealized representative of Anglo-Saxon culture.[44]

According to a dominant strain of nineteenth-century thought, therefore, if Shakespeare's works epitomize the best of English literary creativity and morality, then it stands to reason that his heroines must be implicated in the construction of idealized womanhood. Here and there appeared dissenting views, especially strong later in the century, as women's opportunities expanded. The German scholar Gervinus, whose *Shakespeare Commentaries* were translated into English, had early voiced the opinion that Ophelia is "not without guilt in the fate which meets her" (581), while Ruskin had asserted that she is the only "weak woman" in Shakespeare.[45] Madeleine Leigh-Noel's comment that Ophelia failed Hamlet at his moment of need echoes Ruskin and is reiterated by Jessie Fremont O'Donnell and Laura Stubbs. Using a newer psychological approach, Stubbs sees Ophelia as "the victim of a hyper-sensitive nature . . . too highly-strung and too terse to be a fitting complement to Hamlet"; while O'Donnell calls her "much over-rated . . . a simple shallow girl."[46] The mythos of Ophelia as the quintessential injured innocent, however, has been too strong to die away. While her figure may no longer be spiritualized, nevertheless it retains a magnetism that continues to draw many into its tragic beauty.

Notes

[1] Helena Faucit Martin, *On Some of Shakespeare's Female Characters*, 5th ed (Edinburgh: Blackwood, 1893) 4.

[2] *Friendship's Offering* (London, 1836): 253.

[3] Victorian men in particular seem to have been fascinated by the idea of capturing that moment right before a young girl opens into full womanhood and the death of innocence. Ruskin and Carroll most obviously come to mind. Jeffrey Stern writes that for Lewis Carroll and the Pre-Raphaelites, "growing up is itself a kind of death"— a moment "of anguish rather than liberation. . . . it does not seem coincidence that Shakespeare's Ophelia, the archetypal doomed virgin-heroine, was painted by no less than three of the artists whom Carroll knew and admired. . . . in so doing, Hughes, Rossetti, and Millais were all fired by a vision of threatened virgin beauty . . . ." "The death of Ophelia, or the metamorphosis of Alice from childhood to adulthood, are ways in which such a personal inevitability can be entertained in its most pleasing — because controlled — form . . . ." Jeffrey Stern, "Lewis Carroll the Pre-Raphaelite 'Fainting in Coils,'" *Lewis Carroll Observed*, ed. Edward Guiliano (New York: Potter, 1976) 177–178.

[4] Anna Jameson, *Characteristics of Women . . .*, 3rd ed, vol. 1 (London: Saunders and Otley, 1835) 253.

[5] Jameson 254.

[6] Jameson 255.

[7] Jameson 258–59.

[8] Jameson 260.

[9] Jameson 272.

[10] Jameson 279.

[11] Jameson 279.

[12] References to *Hamlet* are from The Arden Shakespeare, edited by Harold Jenkins (London: Methuen, 1982).

[13] Madeleine Leigh-Noel, *Shakspeare's Garden of Girls* (London: Remington, 1885) 151.

[14] Martin 13.

[15] Louis Lewes, *The Women of Shakespeare*, trans. Helen Zimmern (New York: Putnam's; London: Hodder, 1895) 276–77. Lewes was obviously influenced by Jameson who wrote that when Ophelia "is brought to the court, she seems, in her loveliness and perfect purity, like a seraph that had wandered out of bounds, and yet breathed on earth the air of paradise" (112).

[16] An Actress, *The True Ophelia . . .* (London: Sidgwick, 1913) 19.

[17] An Actress 24–25.

[18] See R. Chris Hassel, "Painted Women: Annunciation Motifs in *Hamlet*," *Comparative Drama* 32 (1998-99): 47; and Bridget Gellert Lyons, "The Iconography of Ophelia," *ELH* 44 (1977): 60-74.

[19] Hassel 48.

[20] William Michael Rossetti, *Dante Gabriel Rossetti. His Family Letters with a Memoir*, vol. 1 (London, 1895; New York: AMS, 1970) 367.

[21] For representations of most of these images, see the Rossetti Archive Website at the University of Virginia: http://jefferson.village.virginia.edu/rossetti/index.html

[22] See Rossetti's 1850 painting, *Ecce Ancilla Domini*, done slightly before the *Hamlet*, where the Virgin presses herself back against the wall, indicating fear of the Angel. Rossetti's sister Christina was a model for the Virgin. See Jan Marsh, *Pre-Raphaelite Women* (London: Artus, 1994) 32.

[23] Harry Rusche, Commentary on "Dante Gabriel Rossetti, *Hamlet and Ophelia*, 1858," in the *Shakespeare Illustrated* Website: www.emory.edu/ENGLISH/classes/Shakespeare_Illustrated/Rossetti.Hamlet.html.

[24] Rusche, Web Commentary.

[25] Lewes 276–77.

[26] In Folger Library collection, Art Vol. a34 vol. 17

[27] Lewes 278.

[28] An Actress 48, 58–59.

[29] Folger Library collection, shelf mark Art Vol. f67.

[30] Other Pre-Raphaelite paintings with similar frames include: Ford Maddox Brown, *The First Translation of the Bible into English* 1848; Holman-Hunt, *Valentine Rescuing Sylvia* 1850–51 (illustrating Shakespeare's *Two Gentlemen of Verona*); and his *The Finding of the Saviour in the Temple* 1854–60. Hughes was a friend of both of these artists. Elaine Showalter notes particularly in Hughes's picture, that "the straw in her hair resembles a crown of thorns." She describes his depiction of Ophelia as a "juxtaposition of childlike femininity and Christian martyrdom." (Elaine Showalter, "Representing Ophelia: Women, Madness and the Responsibilities of Feminist Criticism," *Shakespeare and the Question of Theory*, ed. Patricia Parker and Geoffrey Hartman [New York: Methuen, 1985] 85).

[31] Exhibited at the Royal Academy in 1831. Collections of portraits of beautiful women, real or fictional, were popular in the nineteenth century and were published in such books as *Female Portraits of the Court of Queen Victoria* (1839), *Finden's Byron Beauties* (1836) or Charles Heath's *Shakespeare Gallery* (1836). John Bostock's two paintings of Ophelia (one for Charles Heath's *Gallery*) follow in this tradition.

[32] Location unknown. Exhibited at the British Institution in 1849.

[33] At the Oakland Museum, Oakland, California.

[34] While most artists depict Ophelia dressed in white, noted exceptions are Rossetti's 1868 watercolor, *The First Madness of Ophelia* (Oldham Art Gallery, England) where she wears a blue tunic, and J. W. Waterhouse's 1910 painting of her (Pre-Raphaelite, Inc., London) dressed in a violet-blue gown with gold border. Ellen Terry wanted to wear black when she played Ophelia in 1878 to indicate that the girl was in mourning after the death of her father, Polonius, but she was told, "'My God! Madam, there must be only one black figure in this play, and

that's Hamlet!'" (Ellen Terry, *The Story of My Life* [New York: Schocken Books, 1982] 100).

[35] From *The Athenaeum*, 22 May, 1852, quoted in Richard Altick, *Paintings from Books* (Columbus: Ohio State University Press, 1985) 301.

[36] See Sandra M. Donaldson, "Ophelia in Elizabeth Siddal Rossetti's Poem 'A Year and A Day,'" *Journal of Pre-Raphaelite Studies* 2.1 (1981): 127-33; and Marsh 140.

[37] Quoted from Carolyn Hares-Stryker, ed. *An Anthology of Pre-Raphaelite Writings* (New York: New York University Press, 1997) 96.

[38] The male and female views are nicely contrasted in two paintings of the early twentieth century. Margaret MacDonald's symbolist watercolor (1908; Private Collection) of a stylized Ophelia, floating on water, is both ethereal and disturbing. Four white angel-like heads hover over the smiling Ophelia with roses in her hair, but she floats bare-breasted, and the side of her gown turns to a scaled tail, as though she were becoming a mermaid. At the other extreme is W. G. Simmonds's 1910 watercolor in a more realistic style, showing a blond Ophelia at the moment of falling into the water, her white robes billowing out like angel's wings. (*The Tragedy of Hamlet*, Illus. W.G. Simmonds [London: Hodder & Stoughton, 1910]).

[39] See Christine Poulson, "Death and the Maiden: The Lady of Shalott and the Pre-Raphaelites," *Re-framing the Pre-Raphaelites . . .*, ed. Ellen Harding (Aldershot, ENG; Brookfield, VT: Scolar P, 1996) 173–194.

[40] See the print by Gustav Dreher after Trentacoste's sculpture, Folger Library shelf mark Black Box Romeo and Juliet (in the exhibition but not illustrated).

[41] Elisabeth Bronfen, *Over Her Dead Body . . .* (New York: Routledge, 1992) 11.

[42] Bronfen 110.

[43] Kaara Peterson, "Framing Ophelia: Representation and the Pictorial Tradition," *Shakespearean Criticism* 48: Yearbook 1998 (Detroit: Gale, 2000) 261.

[44] See Tricia Lootens, *Lost Saints: Silence, Gender, and Victorian Literary Canonization* (Charlottesville: University Press of Virginia, 1996) on the Victorian idealization of Shakespeare.

[45] John Ruskin, "Of Queens' Gardens," *Sesame and Lilies* (London: Allen, 1904) 95.

[46] Jessie Freemont O'Donnell, "Ophelia," *The American Shakespeare Magazine* 3 (March 1897) and Laura Stubbs, "That Shakespeare's Women Are Ideals," *The Stratford-upon-Avon Herald*, July 1898, both as cited in *Women Reading Shakespeare: 1660–1900*, ed. Ann Thompson and Sasha Roberts (Manchester and New York: Manchester University Press, 1997) 248, 241.

Figure 47
Jean Simmons as Ophelia in **Hamlet***,* 1948
Promotional Still
Hamlet, 1948, Laurence Olivier, Director
Released by Universal International Pictures
Two Cities Film, J. Arthur Rank enterprise
Courtesy Photofest, Inc.

Ophelia in Performance in the Twentieth Century

H. R. Coursen

University of Maine, Augusta

his essay will argue that the role of Ophelia is central to *Hamlet*. I will defend that thesis by looking at several Ophelias of the twentieth century — many of which I have seen — and by suggesting that the range of options available to the actor playing Ophelia informs us centrally about how we are to interpret the play swirling around her. Certainly, she tells the inner world of the play what Elsinore is all about. Her truth, though, like that of the poet, comes at both us and Elsinore "slantwise" and therefore implicates us profoundly in the process of interpretation. We are bound, then, to disagree about the character and the nature of the world that destroys her.

The Ophelia Shakespeare wrote is much more than Laertes's "rose of May." Directors can cut Rosencrantz and Guildenstern, as Olivier does in his film, and can eliminate Fortinbras, as Zeffirelli does in his film. Who, after all, is going to take over for Mel Gibson? They can cut the Graveyard scene, as did F. Curtis Canfield at Amherst in 1951 and Luivi Ciulei at Arena Stage in 1978. But if Ophelia is, as the early twentieth-century critic Levin Schucking claims "a beautiful dramatic luxury . . . superfluous" to Shakespeare's design,[1] try editing her out of the play. Schucking had never edited the script for performance.

The script shows that Ophelia is, however unwillingly, a central player in Elsinore's game of espionage. Furthermore, once Hamlet is off on his sea adventure, she takes on his role as Denmark's jester, a singer of songs, a teller of truths, a respondent to the repressed system Claudius has established. Since she is unlicensed, she represents a danger to the kingdom, a palpable manifestation of the sickness raging around this usurped throne, that incestuous bed. Her role as jester is signaled to us, in case we missed it, by her interment in Yorick's grave. We learn there, at grave's edge, that she might have become Queen of Denmark had events turned out differently. She signals, then, the happy ending with which Shakespearean tragedy always entices us.

Furthermore, Ophelia fulfills one of the depth structures of the play, that of the corrupted ritual: from the changing of the guard at the outset (which goes awry because the wrong soldier issues the challenge), to a marriage tinged with memories of a different rite of passage ("Thrift, thrift, Horatio, the funeral bak'd meats did coldly furnish forth the marriage tables"), to a ghost claiming he was murdered before he could enjoy the benefits of last rites, to Hamlet's failed effort to elicit public confession from Claudius, to Claudius's inability to pray, to the hugger-mugger interment of Polonius, to the denial of absolution to Rosencrantz and Guildenstern, to the use of a poisoned chalice to confer damnation on a dying man ("Here, thou incestuous, murd'rous, damned Dane"), to a new reign that begins, as so many new reigns do, with a funeral, where a dead prince's body confers validity to the body politic of a new king. Ophelia's death — as she sings hymns on down the river ("old lauds," in the Second Quarto) — is a reverse baptism. She sinks to muddy death and possible damnation, instead of rising cleansed to newness of life and the promise of salvation. Her funeral rites are themselves "maim'd" and marred by Laertes's quarrel with the Priest and then by one of those brawls that most of us try to avoid at weddings, funerals, and other solemn events. Suffice it that Denmark is cut off by regicide from the encompassing and positive powers of the grace of God. That is an old-fashioned interpretation, of course, but Shakespeare was not writing to conform to post-modernist tenets. Ophelia — who might have been a medium through which positive energies and future princes could become available to Denmark — becomes just another victim. Her story reflects the tragedy of Hamlet. I say, tragedy, because Hamlet has choices and makes them. Ophelia, like the rest of Elsinore, is subject to the errors in judgment that the Prince commits. While the range of her performance is limited — she has only 169 lines (Hamlet has almost 1500) — that range is wide. Elaine Showalter suggests a cubist Ophelia — a vibrating set of possibilities emerging from the center line, the lines in the play — but taking on many shapes as she descends the staircase of time and of imagination.[2]

It is worth defining the moment in which Ophelia is trapped and from which she will not escape. Her madness more than hints at violation and betrayal — whether her relationship with Hamlet has been consummated or not — but it does not incorporate jealousy. In other words, Ophelia sings of first love, and loss of love, but not of one of the usual reasons for that loss — its interception by another person. The instant of loss is precisely defined, and it is the more painful for its having no reason. Jealousy is a terrible emotion, of course, but what Ophelia is responding to is an inexplicable death of love.

Ophelia is a victim in the play, and she has to be played that way. Some strategies, though, keep her from being merely a product of what male critics of the play and male characters within the play say of her.

Response to victimization after all varies, and that variable is built into the role. She must go mad, of course, but it is up to the actor to chart the course to that madness and to show who Ophelia is and might have been *through* that madness. I think that the script suggests that her so-called "suicide" is an assertive act on her part. As the Gravedigger says, she "willfully seeks her own salvation." The Norton editor, Stephen Greenblatt, says that is "probably a mistake."[3] No. The Gravedigger has always been right. She kills herself in self-defense.

One of the most victimized Ophelias ever has to be Lilly Jacobssen in the Svend Gade silent film of 1920. Hamlet is a woman disguised as a man (Asta Nielsen) and she, of course, falls in love with Horatio (Heinz Stieda). Horatio falls in love with Ophelia. That is an unusual triangle — for this script, at least. To compete for Horatio, Hamlet must woo Ophelia. It is only at the end, after Hamlet has died, that Horatio realizes that the Prince had been a woman all along. Horatio kisses the dead lips, an *ex post facto* recognition of the nature of Hamlet's love for him and his for this sudden and belated she. In that the throne of Denmark requires a king, as this film interprets the election, this Ophelia *and* this Hamlet can be said to be victims of patriarchal attitudes.

In a post-modernist Polish production of 1989, directed by Andrzej Wajda, a woman (Teresa Budcisc-Krzyzanowska) played Hamlet as neither male nor female, but as an actor playing Hamlet, so that the erotic energies of the script were intellectualized. Ophelia (Dorota Segda) was, in this heavily meta-dramatic interpretation, the victim of the words and actions dictated by the script. The struggle lay in Hamlet's effort to survive ("To be"), which he did for awhile, only to have Fortinbras fall into Hamlet's role at the end. The play becomes a repeated imitation of an action in time in which only the names change. The existential dilemma of life before death perpetuates itself, and characters like Ophelia are inevitable victims within the endlessly reiterated narrative.[4] Within this infinite regress and projection of futility, distinctions such as gender become irrelevant.

The first Freudian Ophelias were, almost simultaneously, Rosalind Fuller in New York in 1922 in the Barrymore production and Muriel Hewitt opposite Colin Keith-Johnston in the modern dress production in London in 1925. Fuller was perhaps the first Ophelia to zero in on Claudius with "Young men will do it, if they come to it," as many Ophelias have done since. Hewitt

Figure 48
*Jean Simmons as Ophelia in **Hamlet**,* 1948
Promotional Still
Hamlet, 1948, Laurence Olivier, Director
Released by Universal International Pictures
Two Cities Film, J. Arthur Rank enterprise
Courtesy Photofest, Inc.

Silent film star Lillian Gish (frontispiece, fig. 24) played Ophelia at 40 opposite Gielgud at the Empire Theater in New York in 1936. This is the production that competed successfully for hegemony against the simultaneous Leslie Howard *Hamlet* at the Imperial (with Pamela Stanley as Ophelia and Celeste Holm beginning her career as an extra). The publicity for the former production paired Gielgud with Judith Anderson (Gertrude) above the play's title, and Gish with Arthur Byron (Polonius) below the title. The tension within the role is illustrated by several conflicting approaches to Gish's version. The critics tended to see her conventionally: she displayed a "girlish tenderness" and looked "flower-like" and "a wistful twenty."[5] Gish, however, said that she did not want to make her character "too sweet and childlike" or create "scenes which seem like a sweet old ballad," but to depict "a girl crazed with disillusionment and grief."[6] Gish told Marvin Rosenberg that Gielgud "wanted a 'lewd' Ophelia," but that "she balanced conscious sweetness with eruptions of a repressed unconscious."[7] The case for the older Ophelia is made by Ethel Barrymore, who had essayed the role in 1925: if played by a "little fibbertigibbet," Ophelia's madness will not produce "the shock which Shakespeare meant the audience to feel."[8]

The rebellious Ophelia appears on stage as early as Glenda Jackson opposite David Warner in 1965. She was loud and defiant, and her suicide was seen by critics as a last, rebellious gesture. Gertrude's description of it became, then, an effort to enclose the act within conventional pastoral and religious formats. Since Ophelia had been a stereotypic "rose of May," a projection of male attitudes, when male critics had gone to school and read *Hamlet*, the critics could not deal with Glenda's version. She was "shrewish," "strong-willed," "tough," and "frigidly spinsterish." This was not Dr. Johnson's Ophelia, "the young, the beautiful, the harmless, and the pious," whose "mournful distraction … fills the heart with tenderness."[9] Glenda came on with a guitar and sang her songs as if at a protest rally. The only woman who reviewed Jackson, Penelope Gilliat, thought she should have played Hamlet.[10] She was asked to do so, later, but made the film "House Calls" instead.

The great film director, Grigori Kozintsev, emerging from Stalinist Russia, puts political weight on Ophelia. Her "madness is a social event. People . . . look for a secret meaning in [her gibberish]. The government reels. The mad woman is a sign of disaster."[11] According to

played her mad scenes erotically in a flimsy gown, setting in motion a thousand Ophelias for whom going bonkers can be accomplished only in that night gown. In each instance, the bawdiness of the lines was kept in, instead of decorously edited out to suggest the finer-than-Elizabethan Victorian sensibilities.

The conventional Ophelia is exemplified by Jean Simmons (figs. 47, 48) in the influential Olivier film of the late 1940s. It is worth noting, however, that she is the only character in the film who has a contact with nature. She lives in a flowered chamber suffused with light and opening out into the gardens of comedy, in contrast to the stony shadows of the castle. Her death under trees and amid flowers is grimly appropriate. At one point, Hamlet puts a blonde wig on the boy actor, who looks back at him and looks exactly like Ophelia. Hamlet knows what he is seeing, but rejects it, perhaps hinting at a drowning of his own androgyny as he shakes off the image presented so innocently to him.

Figure 49
*Julia Stiles as Ophelia in **Hamlet**,* 2000
Promotional Still
Hamlet, 2000, Michael Almereyda, Director
Miramax Films

Elsinore. "Set your entreatments at a higher rate/Than a command to parley," says Polonius to Ophelia. It would seem that Gertrude moves easily within this system of exchange with her philosophy that all kings look alike in the dark. Some Gertrudes suggest that Claudius is preferable to the militaristic former king, who wore his armor to bed. The contrast between the two men is drawn by John Updike in his recent *Gertrude and Claudius.* Whatever Gertrude learns, she learns late what Ophelia learns too soon and, of course, too late.

In the Ciulei production of 1978 at the Arena Stage in Washington, Christine Estabrook's Ophelia smashed in on a state dinner party. Ophelia must interact imaginatively with the script and with the world of her production. She is not a reverent reader of the lines or a wan off-key singer, à la Lalla Ward for BBC in 1980 or Kate Winslet for Branagh in 1996. Ragnar Lyth's superb 1984 Ophelia (Pernilla Wallgren) interrupts a state reception, demanding "Where is the beauteous majesty of Denmark?" and has to be hustled away. Later, as Laertes and Hamlet grapple, her body tumbles out of its coffin into the mud of her grave. Even in death, she is victimized by the games the boys are playing. In the Almereyda film of 2000, Julia Stiles (fig. 49) plays the rebellious Ophelia powerfully. Her scream replicates the circular walkway of the Guggenheim and rattles around in the atrium below, a version of her descent into a psychic maelstrom. She dies in a pool under a fountain, Hamlet's letters scattered around her. Samuel Crowl finds here an allusion to Keats's epitaph in the Protestant Cemetery in Rome. "Here lies one whose name was writ in water."[18] The words on the letters themselves have melted into the recycled system of the fountain. Since they represented to Ophelia "almost all the holy vows of heaven," their erasure here hints at the anti-baptismal moment that Ophelia's drowning represents. Truth has become a liar, to paraphrase one of Hamlet's letters to her. If Almereyda intends the allusion to Keats, it is appropriate as a gesture toward a failed love affair and youthful death.

Ophelia is sometimes imaged as ghost, as is Ciaran Madden in the 1970 television version with Richard Chamberlain. Wrapped in a sheet, she resembles John Gielgud's wispy King Hamlet. In her mad scenes in the Tony Richardson film of 1969, Marianne Faithfull's (fig. 50) pale face brings a ghostly presence to a production that doesn't have a visible Ghost. Faithfull's songs are words from the dead. A young maid's wits are as mortal, after all, as an old man's life. According to Robert Brustein, Ingmar Bergman's Ophelia, Pernilla

this reading, she, like the Ghost "bodes some strange eruption to [the] state." "Her madness has a narrative meaning, and its subject is Claudius's court," says Michael Pennington.[12] Furthermore, as Karin S. Coddon suggests, "in the ambiguous space where reason and madness intersect lies treason,"[13] and treason lies in word as well as action. "My brother shall know of it," Ophelia says. She, too, "is a kind of revenger," says Michael Cohen.[14] Ophelia's songs are hardly irrelevant snatches. Women in early modern times, says Diane Purkiss, are beginning to be seen "as the bearers of a subversive popular culture which challenged the high."[15] Bert O. States suggests that Ophelia manifests a dangerous, if latent, sexuality that must be controlled.[16] Kathleen McLuskie, speaking of *Measure for Measure,* says that women are "objects of exchange within [a] system of sexuality."[17] And that is certainly true of

Figure 50
*Marianne Faithfull as
Ophelia in* **Hamlet**, 1969
Promotional Still
Hamlet, 1969, Tony
Richardson, Director
A Woodfall Production/
Columbia Pictures
Courtesy Photofest, Inc.

Figure 51
*Anatasia Vertinskaya
as Ophelia in* **Gamlet
[Hamlet]**, 1964
Promotional Still
Hamlet, 1964, Grigori
Kozintsev, Director
Lenfilm
Courtesy Photofest, Inc.

Ostergren, "appears at the rainy funeral ceremony that follows her death. [She] materializes at the back, in bare feet, blue slip, and flowered crown — now a ghost haunting her own burial service."[19] Kenneth Branagh describes the drowned Ophelia as "a beautiful ghostly corpse."[20]

Some of the radical differences in representing Ophelias on film are manifested by Anastasia Vertinskaya, Faithfull, and Helena Bonham-Carter.

In Kosintsev's great 1964 film, the striking Vertinskaya is, in sanity, tightly bound and rigidly choreographed (fig. 51). In madness, her hair is down, her gown is loose, and she is eerily ecstatic. Kozintsev

Figure 52
Helena Bonham-Carter as Ophelia in **Hamlet**, 1990
Promotional Still
Hamlet, 1990, Franco Zeffirelli, Director
Warner Bros. Pictures
Courtesy Photofest, Inc.

says that "madness is happiness for Ophelia."[21] She also moves like an old woman, as if arthritis has settled into the limbs so robotized earlier. Yet she does move, weaving in and out of the static soldiers of Laertes's rebellion, suggesting that she has gained an ironic mobility within a rigid, militaristic world.

As Laertes lectures Faithfull's Ophelia about Hamlet in the Richardson film, she begins to laugh at his priggish lines. They are having an incestuous affair, and he is saying in a man's usual awkward way, save it for me. The subtext of her response is — Oh — you want me to

keep my legs crossed? Then don't pull a double standard on me! It is a wonderful moment, but it renders Ophelia's relationship with Hamlet a trivial dalliance in the midst of a long-term affair with her brother.

In the Zeffirelli film of 1990, Bonham-Carter (fig. 52) is an intelligent Ophelia, Hamlet's intellectual soul mate. You know that she can keep up with him in debate. In a magnificent moment in this film, which so effectively places faces in front of architecture, Bonham-Carter calls for her coach and begins to exit. She pauses for a moment, her swollen eyes surrounded by the inside of the keep of the castle. It forms a giant crown over her head. She becomes for a moment, Queen Ophelia of Denmark. It is only a slight stretch to suggest that the great, radiating circle above her also becomes a halo, emblem of Ophelia's martyrdom to the murderous power of Elsinore.

Kenneth Branagh's film of 1996 suggests Ophelia's danger to the state. Kate Winslet is excruciating, a victim of a director who gives her nothing but her lines. When Derek Jacobi's Claudius appears, however, he recognizes that the scene is about *him* and that any effort he makes in the direction of humanity compromises his fragile political position. The production misses a magnificent opportunity by not having Ophelia die of the cold water treatments to which she is subjected in what the script for the film calls "The Wash Down Cell."[22] Gertrude's pretty speech would become the "official" version that Laertes would be forced to accept. Instead, this Ophelia has secreted a key in her mouth so that she can get to the miniature icebergs floating through the winter outside the gates. I am surprised that no director has ever had Claudius signal the dispatch of Ophelia — perhaps even handing a parchment to Gertrude, containing her "willow" speech to read to Laertes.

Valerie Von Volz's magnificent Ophelia at Monmouth in 1979 was beginning to go mad at the outset. The atmosphere of Elsinore was already affecting one of its more sensitive citizens. Her first appearance — tall, dark, eyes edging into wildness, a kind of Madeline Usher — made the audience gasp. This Ophelia permitted one to understand why some critics suggest that Hamlet's interruption of her sewing, as she reports it to Polonius, never really occurred.[23]

Frances Barker, who played Ophelia opposite Roger Rees for the Royal Shakespeare Company in 1984, sees "Ophelia as a female counterpart to the Prince" driven mad by "her powerlessness to prevent what she sees."[24] The prose and songs of her mad scenes are a way of breaking free of the controlled beat of Claudius's court — "Though yet of Hamlet, our dear brother's death,/ The memory be green." A good moment occurred in that RSC production as a disconsolate Ophelia wandered off after the Nunnery Scene (Act III, scene 1). The Boy Actor entered and stared at her, as if recognizing another person forced to play a role that proclaimed against identity. The moment made a thematic transition between scenes and brought together two characters seldom linked. It also reminded us that all the women in the plays had once been played by boys.

In a 1994 production at Stratford, Ontario, the older generation, Claudius and Gertrude, went about things quite happily, as if the kingdom had suffered only minor tremors. The element of feeling had flowed into the younger generation. The production developed the distinction between generations that Zeffirelli's late 1960s film of *Romeo and Juliet* depicts so brilliantly. Hamlet (Stephen Ouimette) lashed out at Ophelia (Sabrina Grdevich) with his anger at Gertrude. Ophelia became the stereotypic "my lady," who paints an inch thick. The Nunnery Scene was an extension of the scene that Ophelia had described earlier for Polonius, but it was not an effort by Hamlet to broadcast his "antic disposition." It was blind rage. Hamlet lacerated the person most like him in the play — Ophelia. His excoriation signaled his own doom, coming as it did from a repressed self, from a denial of something in himself that he might have recognized and loved, an energy his feelings toward his mother had distorted. Ophelia needed that recognition and love for her own completion. Central to Hamlet's tragedy is his inability to maintain his relationship with Ophelia. Here, that failure was not a function of Elsinore's poisonous atmosphere. That he did not recognize his natural ally in that world was Hamlet's fault.

The independent Ophelia was exemplified by Dawn Lissell in the Ashland, Oregon production of 1994. In the Nunnery Scene, she made a desperate attempt to communicate with Richard Howard's Hamlet, saying the lines but trying to refute them with gestures. "There, my lord" was supposed to suggest to the eavesdroppers that she was returning gifts. Actually, she pointed to where Claudius and Polonius hid. Hamlet, however, instead of being grateful for her confiding in him, grew angry when he realized they were being spied upon. Ophelia's "At home, my lord" was a line in a play that she was agreeing to play since they had an audience. Lissell let out an agonized cry when she realized that her efforts to communicate with Hamlet had failed. Her soliloquy at the end of the scene became a powerful expression of her own loss. Later, in her madness, her "we must be patient" imitated her gruff father's advice. Resentment had flowed in to replace hope. She played the past in her madness, and the scenes had an eerie sense of Lady Macbeth at the beginning of Act Five of that play.

An equally assertive Ophelia was that of Asch Gregory in Portland, Maine in 1994. Her report to Polonius implicated her in a political plot of which she wanted no part. She could establish "body natural" — that is the person beneath the politics — only in madness. Her identity and grasp of reality had been driven inward so that her songs and distribution of flowers emerged from an inviolable core of being. She moved intently into her role, insisting that others play the parts she assigned. Both who she was and how Elsinore had denied that self a role were powerfully expressed. Her death was the ultimate expression of her singularity as well as an indictment of Elsinore. And of course, these motives — one personal and one political — express the cancellation that Ophelia suffers in the script.

Lissell developed roles for herself from the fragments of her psyche. Gregory assigned roles to others from those same fragments. The irony of Ophelia's madness, Pennington suggests, lies in Ophelia's "undeceived vision of the world around her — the last thing we expected of this submissive timid girl."[25] Furthermore, her insanity incorporates a clarity that we do not usually attribute to madness.

In the 2000 Odyssey production, the African-American Ophelia, Lisa Gay Hamilton, is superb in her mad scene. A lonely "other" in a white world, she actually comforts Gertrude: "We must be patient." She emphasizes Gertrude's own isolation from the killing politics swirling around the women of the court. Convincing as an alien driven into her own psyche by her isolation, Hamilton is not plausible earlier in the late nineteenth or early twentieth century setting. The relationship between Ophelia and Hamlet is doubtful, particularly for a debonair and shallow prince very unlikely to discern value beneath appearances. Hamlet's attraction to her cannot be written off as an act of rebellion, since she is the daughter of Prime Minister Polonius.

In the 1995 Shenandoah Shakespeare Express production, Michelle Powers was also African-American. This was on stage, though, not film or television. We were asked to suspend our disbelief, a contract we are likely to accept as we look at an unadorned stage with no specific time assigned to the script. We yield to individual performance rather than absorb historical contexts that condition and control the words and the gestures. In her mad scene, Powers did a brief Billy Holiday imitation. Powers's inspiration was "God Bless the Chile." It was chilling in its fusion of divergent traditions into one role.

Two brilliant recent Ophelias on stage have been Joanne Pearce and Cathryn Bradshaw. Pearce, in the Adrian Noble production (1992, with Kenneth Branagh) was on the brink of yielding to Hamlet's importunity and would have done so during the nunnery scene, played in her bedroom, had not the king and her father been lurking inconveniently in her wardrobe. Having been thwarted in making the transition from Narnia to womanhood, she played a polonaise on her upright piano. Polonius (David Bradley), however, closed the lid. Ophelia was not to be permitted to escape to childhood after what her father viewed as her vivid failure with the Crown Prince. Madness became her future and she lost her virginity there, rolling on her back and pulling her clothes tight between her legs. That the nunnery scene occurred in her room meant that she had those "remembrances" handy and, thus, overcame the awkward suggestion that she had been lugging them around hoping for a chance encounter with Hamlet. Furthermore, she was *not* lying when she said that Polonius was "at home."

Later, in her madness, she wore the formal clothes in which Polonius had been murdered, blood bright on the white shirt as a displacement of the virginity she would now lose only in mime. She was a Chaplinesque clown in floppy clothes, a "fool" bringing uncomfortable truths to this shallow court. Her face was white, predicting the Golgotha of the graveyard and her taking over of Yorick's restless grave. If we did not know the play, we observed her in that bony light once her funeral train wended into view. She was pulled "bare-fac'd [from] the bier" twice, once by Laertes and once by Hamlet, in death as in life, a puppet in a game of male posturing.

Cathryn Bradshaw in the John Caird production

(2001, with Simon Russell Beale) used Claudius's arm and her own vocal imitation for the door that swung open to admit the "maid" of her song. She imitated the masculine roguishness of the young man's voice ("And thou hadst not come to my bed"). This was the voice of her repressed *animus* — the male component of the feminine psyche — the power that might have countervailed the destructive energies of the male world, the resistance to Polonius's demand that she "think [her]self a baby" emerging too late. This Ophelia broke in on Laertes's rebellion brandishing Polonius's staff. "Beware/Of entrance to a quarrel," she cried from up left, creating a stunning attack of her own. She wore the formal fur-trimmed gown in which Polonius had been killed. As in Pearce's depiction of the role in 1992, the father's clothes signaled at once a wish for protection and the futility of that wish.

Bradshaw simulated Polonius's death and lay down, her hands folded in front of her. She was her father's alter ego, acting out something she understood only physically, and attempting to compensate for the lack of ceremony attendant on Polonius's death. Since Polonius was not played with a beard (Hamlet's "It shall to the barber's with your beard" had been cut earlier), Ophelia's reference to a "beard … white as snow" seemed to be the projection of a conventional old age and natural death into her mimicry. She got up, leaving Polonius's robe and shoes on the imagined grave and dropped fragments of Hamlet's letters on the imagined corpse. The use of the letters for the herbs Ophelia distributes was employed by Diane Venora in the Kevin Kline production of 1990. Here it was poignant because the line "that's for remembrance" was directly linked to a scrap of one of Hamlet's love letters. To complete the sequence, Gertrude dropped her original wedding veil and bouquet on Ophelia's grave, neatly objectifying Gertrude's heartbroken conflation of bride bed and grave. Caird added "maimed rites" to his production, stressing their significance in the inherited scripts.

Hamlet contains its audition pieces for the title role. Michael Redgrave, Michael Pennington, and Kenneth Branagh, for example, graduated from Laertes to the role of Hamlet. Pennington has gone on to double Ghost and Claudius. Sarah Bernhardt played Ophelia and later Hamlet. Probably the only actor to audition for Ophelia by playing Hamlet was Diane Venora, who played the title role for Joseph Papp and Ophelia later in the Kevin Kline production. She graduates to Gertrude in the Almereyda film.

Hamlet cannot always tell us what his play is about. I don't think he knows. Ophelia, though, is a Jamesan reflector — a virgin violated by Elsinore's agenda of espionage, a verbalizer of the kingdom's rampant sexuality, a manifestation of a politics run amuck, a rebellious and possibly treasonous subject of a regicide, the exponent of a ritual behavior that must fail in this kingdom. She moves in time — a still unravished girl, a flower-decked Victorian madwoman, an emancipated flapper, a folk singer at an anti-war rally, an articulate exponent of the feminist movement. She tells us where the play is in time and where we are in history. If we watch Ophelia carefully, we will get a sense of what the production is doing and of who we are as that ever-changing script known as *Hamlet* moves past our eyes and ears on stage or screen. She knows, but she can only communicate her meanings and those of the play in ways that force the audience, like Elsinore, "to move the hearers to collection."

Notes

This essay is dedicated to the late C.L. "Joe" Barber.

[1] Levin Schucking, *Character Problems in Shakespeare's Plays* (Berlin, 1917. English trans., New York, 1922) 172.

[2] Elaine Showalter, "Representing Ophelia: Women, Madness, and the Responsibilities of Feminist Criticism," *Shakespeare and the Question of Theory*, eds. Patricia Parker and Geoffrey Hartman (London: Methuen, 1985): 77–94.

[3] Stephen Greenblatt, ed. *The Norton Shakespeare* (New York: W. W. Norton, 1997): 1740, n. 1 to 5.1.

[4] See James Lusardi, "*Hamlet IV*," *Shakespeare Bulletin*, 8, no 2 (Spring 1990): 21-23.

[5] Marvin Rosenberg, *The Masks of Hamlet* (Newark: University of Delaware Press, 1992) 245.

[6] Rosenberg 245.

[7] Rosenberg 245.

[8] Quoted in Rosenberg 245.

[9] Quoted in Bertrand H. Bronson, ed. *Samuel Johnson* (New York: Holt, Rinehart, and Winston, 1952) 302–03.

[10] Quoted in Anthony Dawson, *Shakespeare in Performance: 'Hamlet'* (Manchester: Manchester University Press, 1995) 144–45.

[11] Grigori Kozintsev, *Shakespeare: Time and Conscience*, trans. Joyce Vining (London: Dennis Dobson, 1967) 218.

[12] Michael Pennington, *'Hamlet': A User's Guide* (New York: Limelight, 1996) 116.

[13] Karin S. Coddon, "'Suche Strange Dessygns': Madness, Subjectivity, and Treason in *Hamlet* and Elizabethan Culture," *Hamlet*, ed., Susan L. Wofford (Boston: Bedford, 1994) 390.

[14] Michael Cohen, *'Hamlet': In My Mind's Eye* (Athens: University of Georgia Press, 1989) 123.

[15] Diane Purkiss, *The Witch in History: Early Modern and Twentieth Century Interpretation* (London: Routledge, 1996) 202.

[16] Bert O. States, *Hamlet and the Concept of Character* (Baltimore: Johns Hopkins University Press, 1992) 129–146.

[17] Kathleen McLuskie, "The Patriarchal Bard," *Political Shakespeare*, eds. Jonathan Dollimore and Alan Sinfield (Manchester: Manchester University Press, 1985) 97.

[18] Samuel Crowl, "*Hamlet*, A Review of the Almereyda Production." *Shakespeare Bulletin*, forthcoming, 2001.

[19] Robert Brustein, "Twenty-First Century *Hamlet*," *The New Republic* (18-25 July 1988): 28.

[20] Kenneth Branagh, ed., *Hamlet* (New York: W. W. Norton, 1996) 141.

[21] Kozintsev 101.

[22] Branagh 133.

[23] See H. R. Coursen, "The Closet Scene," *Approaches to Teaching 'Hamlet'* (New York: Modern Language Association), forthcoming, 2001.

[24] Frances Barker, "Ophelia in *Hamlet*," *Players of Shakespeare 2*, eds. Russell Jackson and Robert Smallwood (Cambridge: Cambridge University Press, 1988) 145.

[25] Pennington 121.

Figure 53
JULES–JOSEPH LEFEBVRE
Ophelia, 1890
Oil on canvas
Museum of Fine Arts, Springfield, MA
Given in Memory of Dwight O. Gilmore by his nephews,
Dwight Gilmore and Edwin S. Gardner

Works in the Exhibition

Works are listed in alphabetical order by name of the artist who designed the image. See Index of Artists for other names. Studio photographs and film stills are listed separately in alphabetical order by name of actor. Dimensions are in inches followed by centimeters; height precedes width.

JOHN AUSTEN
British, 1886–1948

Death of Ophelia, 1922
Pen and ink
15 3/4 x 12 (39.5 x 30.6), image
Illustration for William Shakespeare,
Hamlet, Prince of Denmark.
By London, Selwyn and Blout, 1922.
Folger Shakespeare Library,
Washington, D.C.
Fig. 60

CLAUDE FAIVRE
French
After drawing by **MARIE BASHKIRTSEFF**
Russian, 1858–1884

Ophélie, 1877–1884
Etching
5 1/4 x 8 1/4 (13.4 x 21), image
From *L'Artiste,* Jan. 1887
Folger Shakespeare Library,
Washington, D.C.
Fig. 35

Figure 54
WILLIAM HENRY EGLETON
After drawing by **JOHN BOSTOCK**
Ophelia, 1857
Engraving
Mead Art Museum
PR.XX.68
Photo: Stephen Petegorsky

EUGÈNIA BALCELLS
Spanish, born 1943

"OPHELIA" (variacions sobre una imatge [variations on an image]), 1979
Barcelona
Artist's book
9 1/8 x 12 5/8 (23 x 32), 78 pages
The Museum of Modern Art Library,
New York
Figs. 28, 29

After drawing by **JEAN BAPTISTE BERTRAND (called JAMES)**
French, 1823–1887

Ophélie, 1884
Process print of drawing after painting of 1884
4 3/8 x 6 1/4 (11 x 16), image
Illustrated in *L'Artiste,* June 1884
Fine Arts Library, Harvard College Library
Fig. 13

W. JOSEPH EDWARDS
British, active 1840–1863
After a drawing of 1836 by JOHN BOSTOCK
British, 1826–1869

Ophelia (**Hamlet***. Act IV, scene 5*), after 1836
Engraving
5 13/16 x 4 1/4 (14.8 x 10.8), image
From Charles Heath, *The Shakespeare Gallery,
containing the Principal Female Characters in the
Plays of the Great Poet*, London: Charles Tilt,
1836–37
Folger Shakespeare Library,
Washington, D.C.
Fig. 41

WILLIAM HENRY EGLETON
British, active 1833–1862
After drawing by JOHN BOSTOCK
British, 1826–1869

Ophelia, 1857
Engraving
17 7/8 x 14 3/4 (45.5 x 37.5), plate
Mead Art Museum
PR.XX.68
Fig. 54

ACHILLE JACQUES JEAN-MARIE DEVÉRIA
French, 1800–1857
After drawing by LOUIS BOULANGER
French, 1807–1867

Hamlet, Acte IV, scene 5, 1827
Lithograph, hand colored
7 x 8 3/4 (17.7 x 21.4), image
From the *Album Anglais*. One of 10
illustrations from Shakespeare in F. L.
Moreau, *Souvenirs du Théâtre Anglais
à Paris*, Paris, 1827
Folger Shakespeare Library,
Washington, D.C.
Fig. 15

LOUISE BOURGEOIS
American, born 1911 (France)

Hamlet and Ophelia, 1996–97, published
1997
Five color lithograph
29 1/4 x 41 (74.2 x 104.1)
Mead Art Museum
Purchase with William W. Collins
(Class of 1953) Print Fund
2001.570
Fig. 37

GERALD LESLIE BROCKHURST
British, 1890–1978

Ophelia, 1942
Etching
10 7/8 x 8 5/8 (27.5 x 22), plate
Mead Art Museum
Gift of Edward C. Crossett, Class of 1905
1951.684
Fig. 55

JULIA MARGARET CAMERON
British, 1815–1879 (born in India)

Ophelia Study No. 2, 1867
Albumen print

13 x 10 5/8 (33 x 27.1)
George Eastman House
Fig. 32

JULIA MARGARET CAMERON
British, 1815–1879 (born in India)

Ophelia, 1867
Albumen print
13 3/4 x 10 15/16 (35 x 27.8)
Gernsheim Collection, Harry Ransom
Humanities Research Center
The University of Texas at Austin
Fig. 33

DANIEL BERGER
German, 1744–1824
After drawing of 1778 by
DANIEL NIKOLAUS CHODOWIECKI
German, 1726–1807

*Die Mausfalle. Hamlet. III. Aufsug 2ter
Auftritt* [*The Mousetrap,* **Hamlet***, Act III,
Sc. 2*], 1780
Etching
9 5/8 x 11 1/2 (24.2 x 29), plate
Folger Shakespeare Library,
Washington, D.C.
Fig. 3

GUSTAV DREHER
German, 1856–?
After sculpture by
DOMENICO CRENTACOSTE

Head of Ophelia, c. 1898
Wood engraving
7 1/4 x 9 1/8 (18.3 x 23.2),
plate
Folger Shakespeare Library,
Washington, D.C.

ALAIS
British
After drawing by
GEORGE CRUIKSHANK
British, 1792–1878

Miss Lydia Kelly as Ophelia,
1815
Stipple engraving
5 3/4 x 3 11/16 (14.6 x 9.4),
plate
Caption: "We know what
we are, but we know not
what we may be"
Folger Shakespeare Library,
Washington, D.C.

EUGÈNE DELACROIX
French, 1793–1863

Hamlet et Ophélie (Act. III. Sc. 1)
[*Hamlet and Ophelia*], 1834–1843
Lithograph
10 1/2 x 7 7/8 (24.3 x 19.8), image
First state of two
From the series *Hamlet, Seize sujets
dessinés et lithographiés par Eug. Delacroix*.
Paris, Dusac et Cie., 1864 (not included
in the first edition of 1843 with thirteen
prints)

Folger Shakespeare Library,
Washington, D.C.
Fig. 17

EUGÈNE DELACROIX
French, 1793–1863

*Hamlet fait jouer aux comédiens la scène de
l'empoisonnement de son père (Act. III. Sc. 2)
[Hamlet Has the Actors Play the Scene of his
Father's Poisoning]*, 1835
Lithograph
9 13/16 x 12 3/4 (24.8 x 32. 3), image
Second state of four, printed by Villain
Caption: "C'est une intrigue scélérate, mais
qu'importe? Votre Majesté et nous avons
la conscience libre, Cela ne nous touche en
rien….vous voyez il l'empoisonne dans le
jardin pour s'emparer de son royaume….
l'histoire est réelle, écrite en bel italien."
[Tis a knavish piece of work, but what o'
that? Your majesty, and we that have free
souls, it touches us not…. He poisons him
i'th'garden for his estate….The story is
extant, and written in very choice Italian.
III. 2, 235-257]
From the series *Hamlet. Treize Sujets
Dessinés par Eug. Delacroix*. Paris: Gihaut

Figure 55
GERALD LESLIE BROCKHURST
Ophelia, 1942
Etching
Mead Art Museum
Gift of Edward C. Crossett, Class of 1905
1951.684
Photo: Stephen Petegorsky

Frères, 1843
Folger Shakespeare Library,
Washington, D.C.
Fig. 18

EUGÈNE DELACROIX
French, 1793–1863

Le Chant d'Ophélie (Act. IV. Sc. 5)
[Ophelia's Song], 1834
Lithograph
10 3/16 x 8 3/16 (25.8 x 20.8), image
Second state of five (Delteil 114, iia)
From the series *Hamlet, Seize sujets*

dessinés et lithographiés par Eug. Delacroix.
Paris: Dusac et Cie., 1864 (not included
in the first edition of 1843)
Folger Shakespeare Library,
Washington, D.C.
Fig. 19

EUGÈNE DELACROIX
French, 1793–1863

Mort d'Ophélie (Act. IV. Sc. 7)
[Death of Ophelia], 1843
Lithograph
6 5/16 x 10 1/8 (18.6 x 25.7), image

Between second and third state of four
Caption: "… Ses vêtements appesantis et
trempés d'eau ont entrainé la pauvre
malheureuse." [Till that her garments,
heavy with their drink, Pull'd the poor
wretch…. IV. 3, 180-181]
From the series *Hamlet. Treize Sujets
Dessinés par Eug. Delacroix.* Paris: Gihaut
Frères, 1843
Folger Shakespeare Library,
Washington, D.C.
Fig. 20

EUGÈNE DELACROIX
French, 1793–1863

Hamlet (Ophélie), n.d.
Graphite with brown and black wash
6 3/4 x 3 7/8 (17.3 x 9.7), sheet
Plate facing p. 64 in *Oeuvres Choisies
de Shakspeare.* Traduction entièrement
revue sur le texte anglais par M.
Francisque Michel.
Paris: Firmin Didot frères, fils et Cie
[186-?], extra-illustrated edition
Folger Shakespeare Library,
Washington, D.C.
Fig. 21

HUGH WELCH DIAMOND
British, 1809–1886

*Untitled [Mental Patient, Surrey County
Lunatic Asylum]*
Copy of original albumen print, c. 1851-52
7 x 5 1/2 (17.7 x 14)
By kind permission of the Royal Society of
Medicine, London, England
Fig. 8

THOMAS FRANCIS DICKSEE
British, 1819–1895

Ophelia, 1875
Oil on canvas, 37 x 24 3/4 (94 x 62.9)
Mead Art Museum
Museum Purchase
1961.4
Fig. 1

JEAN ERDMAN
American, born 1917

Ophelia, 1946
Directed and Choreographed by Jean
Erdman
Music by John Cage
Costume by Xenia Cage and Jean Erdman
Videotape of the dance with commentary
by Jean Erdman, excerpt from *Dance and
Myth: The World of Jean Erdman
Part I: The Early Dances,* Nancy Allison,
producer, 1990.

FRANCIS HAYMAN
British, 1708–1776

The Play Scene from Hamlet. [Act III, scene
2], c. 1740–1741
Pen and ink and wash
9 x 6 5/16 (22.6 x 16), sheet
Engraved by Hubert Gravelot (1699–1773)
as Frontispiece to *Hamlet* in *The Works of*

Ophelia

Figure 56
William Henry Mote
After drawing by JOHN HAYTER
*Ophelia (**Hamlet**, Act IV, scene 5),* 1848
Engraving
By Permission of the Folger Shakespeare Library

Mr. William Shakespear.Volume the sixth. Consisting of Tragedies. Oxford, Printed at the Theatre, 1744 (Sir Thomas Hanmer's edition, extra-illustrated, original drawing and engraved frontispiece inserted in vol. 6) Folger Shakespeare Library, Washington, D.C. Fig. 2

WILLIAM HENRY MOTE
British, active 1830–1858
After drawing by JOHN HAYTER
British, 1800–1891

Ophelia (Hamlet, Act IV, scene 5), 1848
Engraving
6 5/8 x 5 1/4 (17 x 13.3), plate
From Charles Heath, *The Heroines of Shakespeare: Comprising the Principal Female Characters in the Plays of the Great Poet*, London, 1848
Folger Shakespeare Library, Washington, D.C.
Fig. 56

CLAUDEL HUOT
Canadian, born 1949

Peter Darling as Ophelia in Robert Lapage's Hamlet, Elsinore, 1997
Silver gelatin print, 1997
8 x 10 (20.3 x 25.5)
Courtesy Ex Machina, Quebec City
Fig. 38

GWEN JOHN
British, 1876–1939

Ophelia: Portrait Imaginé, c. 1910
Black chalk, gray wash touched with white on tan paper
9 7/8 x 8 (25.1 x 20.6)
Yale Center for British Art
Paul Mellon Collection
Fig. 57

JULES-JOSEPH LEFEBVRE
French, 1836–1911

Ophelia, 1890
Oil on canvas
59 1/4 x 36 (150.5 x 91.4)
Museum of Fine Arts, Springfield, Massachusetts
Given in Memory of Dwight O. Gilmore by his nephews, Dwight Gilmore and Edwin S. Gardner
Fig. 53

CHARLES ROLLS
British, c. 1800–1857
After painting by DANIEL MACLISE
British, 1806–1870

The Play Scene from Hamlet, 1842
Engraving
6 1/8 x 10 15/16 (15.5 x 27.8), plate
Folger Shakespeare Library, Washington, D.C.
Fig. 43

MARY ELLEN MARK
American, born 1941

Laurie in the Ward 81 Tub, Oregon State Hospital, 1976
Gelatin silver print
9 x 13 3/8 (23 x 34)
Mead Art Museum
Purchase with Richard Templeton (Class of 1931) Photography Fund
2000.444
Fig. 22

(JOSEPH) KENNY MEADOWS
British, 1790–1874

Untitled [The Death of Ophelia], 1846
Wood engraving
4 3/4 x 3 1/2 (12 x 9) image
Text illustration, p. 187, William Shakespeare, *Prince of Denmark*, London, 1846
Folger Shakespeare Library, Washington, D.C.
Fig. 61

ANNA MASSEY LEA MERRITT
British/American, 1844–1930

Portrait of Ellen Terry as Ophelia, 1879
Etching
9 1/2 x 6 1/2 (23. 6 x 16. 5), plate
First state
Museum of Fine Arts, Boston
Gift of Sylvester Rosa Koehler, K1612

ANNA MASSEY LEA MERRITT
British/American, 1844–1930

Ophelia, 1880
Etching
9 x 7 (23 x 17.4), plate
First trial proof
Museum of Fine Arts, Boston
Gift of Sylvester Rosa Koehler, K1617
Fig. 10

JOHN HAMILTON MORTIMER
British, 1740–1779

Ophelia (Act IV, scene 7), 1775
Black charcoal drawing
13 1/2 x 10 15/16 (34.3 x 27.8)
After the etching in Mortimer's set of twelve prints, *Shakespeare's Characters: Series of Heads*, 1775-76
Folger Shakespeare Library, Washington, D.C.
Fig. 7

WALTER PETERHANS
American, 1897–1960 (born in Germany)

Hommage à Rimbaud ou Ophelia [Homage to Rimbaud or Ophelia], 1929 (printed 1977)
Gelatin silver print
8 9/16 x 9 7/16 (21.8 x 24)
The Saint Louis Art Museum
Gift of Sander Gallery, Inc.
Fig. 16

FRIEDRICH AUGUST MORITZ RETZSCH
German, 1779–1857

Ophelia (Hamlet, Act IV, sc. 5), 1828
Graphite drawing
6 7/8 x 8 13/16 (17.4 x 22.4)
For Retzsch's series of line engravings, *Hamlet*, 1828
Folger Shakespeare Library, Washington, D.C.
Fig. 44

PIERRE ANTOINE BRANCHE
French, 1805–?
After FRIEDRICH AUGUST MORITZ RETZSCH
German, 1779–1857

Hamlet. Act III. scene 1, 1828
Etching
2 7/8 x 3 3/4 (7.3 x 9.6), image
From *Galerie de Shakspeare. Dessins pour ses oeuvres dramatiques gravés à l'eau-forte d'après Retzsch, avec des explications traduites de l'allemand du professeur Boettiger. . . .* Hamlet, Paris: Audot, 1828
Folger Shakespeare Library, Washington, D.C.

PIERRE ANTOINE BRANCHE
French, 1805–?
After FRIEDRICH AUGUST MORITZ RETZSCH
German, 1779–1857

Hamlet. Act III. scene 2, 1828
Etching
2 7/8 x 3 3/4 (7.3 x 9.6), image
From *Galerie de Shakspeare. Dessins pour ses oeuvres dramatiques gravés à l'eau-forte d'après Retzsch, avec des explications traduites de l'allemand du professeur Boettiger. . . .* Hamlèt, Paris: Audot, 1828
Folger Shakespeare Library, Washington, D.C.

PIERRE ANTOINE BRANCHE
French, 1805–?
After FRIEDRICH AUGUST MORITZ RETZSCH
German, 1779–1857

Hamlet. Act IV. scene 5, 1828
Etching
2 7/8 x 3 3/4 (7.3 x 9.6), image
From *Galerie de Shakspeare. Dessins pour ses oeuvres dramatiques gravés à l'eau-forte d'après Retzsch, avec des explications traduites de l'allemand du professeur Boettiger… .* Hamlet, Paris: Audot, 1828
Folger Shakespeare Library, Washington, D.C.

CHARLES GRIGNION
British, 1717–1810
After JAMES ROBERTS
British, 1753–1809

Mrs. [Jane] Lessingham in the character of Ophelia, 1775
Engraving, transferred on Liverpool delft tile, c. 1777–1780
From Bell's edition of Shakespeare, 1775

Figure 57
GWEN JOHN
Ophelia: Portrait Imaginé, c. 1910
Black chalk, gray wash touched with white on tan paper
Yale Center for British Art, Paul Mellon Collection

Folger Shakespeare Library,
Washington, D.C.
Fig. 58

SAMUEL JAMES BOUVERIE HAYDON
British, 1815–1891
With the collaboration of FRANCIS
SEYMOUR HADEN
British, 1818–1910
After pen and ink drawing of 1858
by DANTE GABRIEL ROSSETTI
British, 1828–1882

*Hamlet. Act III, scene 1, Ophelia
Returning the Gift to Hamlet,* c. 1880
Etching, printed in dark brown ink
11 1/4 x 9 3/4 (28.5 x 24.6), plate
Sixth state of six
Folger Shakespeare Library,
Washington, D.C.
Fig. 42

LEEANNE SCHMIDT
American, born 1940

Untitled, 1997
Toned gelatin silver print
18 1/2 x 14 3/8 (47 x 34)
Mead Art Museum
Purchase with Wise Fund for Fine Arts
2001.571
Fig. 23

LINDA STARK
American, born 1956

Ophelia Forever, 1999
Oil on canvas on panel
24 x 24 (61.3 x 61.3)
Courtesy of the artist and Angles Gallery
Santa Monica, CA
Private Collection, Glendale, CA
Fig. 39

EDWARD STEICHEN
American, 1879–1973 (born in Luxembourg)

Lillian Gish (1893–1993) as Ophelia, 1936
Gelatin silver print
13 3/4 x 10 3/4 (35 x 27.4)
The Museum of Modern Art, New York
Gift of the photographer
Fig. 24

MARCUS STONE
British, 1840–1921

Ophelia, 1896
Goupilgravure
10 3/4 x 7 11/16 (27.2 x 19.6), image
After painting of 1888
From *The Graphic Gallery of Shakespeare's
Heroines*
Printed in Paris by Goupil for Sampson
Low, Marston & Company, London, 1896
Folger Shakespeare Library,
Washington, D.C.
Fig. 40

JOHN OGBORNE, THE ELDER
British, 1755–c. 1795
After THOMAS STOTHARD
British, 1755–1834

Ophelia, 1783
Etching, engraving and aquatint printed in
light brown
12 x 12 (30.5 x 30.5), diameter of image
Caption: "There's fennel for you and
columbines. There's rue for you"
Inserted before p. 115 in vol. 9, *Hamlet,*
from *The Dramatic works of Shakspear*
revised by George Steevens. London:
Printed by W. Bulmer and Co…. for John
and Josiah Boydell, George and W. Nicol,
from the types of W. Martin, 1802
Folger Shakespeare Library,
Washington, D.C.
Fig. 4

HAROLD SWAHN
American, born 1905

Jean Erdman Dancing Ophelia, 1946
Silver gelatin print
8 x 10 (20.3 x 25.5)
Private Collection of Nancy Allison

MYRON TANNENBAUM
American

Jean Erdman Dancing Ophelia, 1946
Silver gelatin print
8 x 10 (20.3 x 25.5)
Private Collection of Nancy Allison
Fig. 36

FRANCESCO BARTOLOZZI
Italian, 1727–1815
After drawing by HENRY TRESHAM
British, 1751–1814

Ophelia vide Hamlet, 1794
Colored etching
13 1/8 x 18 1/16 (33.3 x 46), plate
Folger Shakespeare Library,
Washington, D.C.
Fig. 6

CHARLES WARREN
British, 1767–1823
After drawing by THOMAS UWINS
British, 1782–1857

Ophelia's Death, 1805
Engraving
5 1/8 x 3 1/8 (13 x 8), image
Folger Shakespeare Library,
Washington, D.C.

Figure 58
CHARLES GRIGNION
After JAMES ROBERTS
Mrs. [Jane] Lessingham in the character of Ophelia, 1775
Engraving, transferred on Liverpool delft tile, c. 1777–1780
By Permission of the Folger Shakespeare Library

AUGUSTE DE VALMONT
French, active 1815–1845

*Mlle Smithson, Rôle d'Offélia dans **Hamlet** (Théâtre Anglais à Paris) [Harriet Smithson as Ophelia in **Hamlet**]*, 1827
Two-toned lithograph, hand colored
7 x 6 1/2 (17.8 x 16.5), image
Caption: " I cannot chuse but weep, to think, they could lay him in the cold ground."
Folger Shakespeare Library, Washington, D.C.
Fig. 14

FRANCIS LEGAT
British, 1755–1809
After painting of 1792 by **BENJAMIN WEST**
American, 1738–1820

Hamlet. Act IV, scene v. Elsinore.–King, Queen, Laertes, Ophelia, & c., 1802
Engraving
19 1/2 x 24 11/16 (49.5 x 62.5), plate
Plate XLV from *A Collection of Prints, from Pictures for the Purpose of Illustrating the Dramatic Works of Shakespeare, by Artists of Great Britain.*
Vol. 1-2. London: John and Josiah Boydell, Shakespeare Gallery.
Printed by W. Bulmer and Co., 1803.
Amherst College
Archives and Special Collections
Fig. 5

RICHARD WESTALL
British, 1765–1836

*Ophelia (**Hamlet**, Act IV, scene 7)*, 1793
Oil on canvas
31 1/8 x 22 1/8 (78.5 x 56)
Collection of Margaret and Henry Erbe
Fig. 12

CHARLES HEATH
British, 1785–1848
After painting by **RICHARD WESTALL**
British, 1765–1836

Hamlet, Act IV, scene 7, Ophelia, before 1848
Engraving
3 3/8 x 2 9/16 (8.6 x 6.5), image
Folger Shakespeare Library, Washington, D.C.

EDWARD SCRIVEN
British, 1775–1841
After drawing by **SAMUEL DE WILDE**
British, 1748–1832

Miss Bolton as Ophelia in Hamlet, 1813
Stipple engraving
8 x 5 1/2 (20.3 x 14)
Folger Shakespeare Library, Washington, D.C.

CHARLES ROLLS
British, 1800–1857
After painting of 1831 by **JOHN WOOD**
British, 1801–1870

Ophelia, after 1831
Engraving
3 15/16 x 2 7/8 (10 x 7.4), image
Folger Shakespeare Library, Washington, D.C.
Fig. 46

UNKNOWN ARTIST
British

Oph: Oh, woe is me! To have seen what I have seen, see what I see.
Hamlet. Act III, scene 1, c. 1830–1850
Wood engraving
7 7/8 x 5 1/4 (20 x 13.5), image
Folger Shakespeare Library, Washington, D.C.

UNKNOWN ARTIST
British

Sarah Siddons (1755–1831) as Ophelia, c. 1785–1786
Pen and ink with brown wash
10 5/8 x 8 (27 x 27.4)
Caption inscribed in pen: "Sarah Siddons as Ophelia
Enter Ophelia fantastically dressed with straws and flowers.
Laertes: Oh heat, dry up my brains! Tears seven times salt, Burn out the sense and virtue of mine eye!…*Hamlet* Act IV"
Folger Shakespeare Library, Washington, D.C.
Fig. 59

*Helena Bonham-Carter as Ophelia in **Hamlet***, 1990
Promotional Still
Hamlet, 1990, Franco Zeffirelli, Director
Warner Bros. Pictures
Courtesy Photofest
Fig. 52

*Marianne Faithfull as Ophelia in **Hamlet***, 1969
Promotional Still
Hamlet, 1969, Tony Richardson, Director
A Woodfall Production/Columbia Pictures
Courtesy Photofest
Fig. 50

Julia Marlowe (1866-1950) as Ophelia, 1904–1924
Photograph
10 x 13 1/4 (25.3 x 33.7)
White, New York
Folger Shakespeare Library, Washington, D.C.

Helena Modjeska (1840–1909) as Ophelia, 1889–90
Carte-de-visite photograph
5 5/8 x 3 15/16 (14.3 x 10)
Edwin Booth Production
Napoleon Sarony, New York
Folger Shakespeare Library, Washington, D.C.

*Kim Novak in **Vertigo***, 1958
Frame enlargement
Vertigo, Alfred Hitchcock, Director/Producer, 1958
Paris, Cinémathèque française collection
© 1958 Universal City Studios, Inc.
All rights reserved
Courtesy of Universal Studios Licensing, Inc.
Fig. 27

*Jean Simmons as Ophelia in **Hamlet***, 1948
Promotional Still
Hamlet, 1948, Laurence Olivier, Director
Released by Universal International Pictures
Two Cities Film, J. Arthur Rank enterprise
Courtesy Photofest
Fig. 47

*Jean Simmons as Ophelia in **Hamlet***, 1948
Promotional Still
Hamlet, 1948, Laurence Olivier, Director
Released by Universal International Pictures
Two Cities Film, J. Arthur Rank enterprise
Courtesy Photofest
Fig. 48

Miss Ellen Terry (1847–1928) as Ophelia, 1878–1904
Carte-de-visite photograph
5 5/8 x 3 15/16 (14.3 x 10)
Window and Grove, London
Folger Shakespeare Library, Washington, D.C.
Fig. 9

*Julia Stiles as Ophelia in **Hamlet***, 2000
Promotional Still
Hamlet, 2000, Michael Almereyda, Director
Miramax Films
Fig. 49

*Anatasia Vertinskaya as Ophelia in **Gamlet** [**Hamlet**]*, 1964
Promotional Still
Hamlet, 1964, Grigori Kozintsev, Director
Lenfilm
Courtesy Photofest
Fig. 51

Sarah Siddons as Ophelia,

Enter Ophelia fantastically dressed with straws and flowers.

Laertes : O heat, dry up my brains ! tears, seven times salt,

Burn out the sense and virtue of mine eye ! ....

Hamlet. Act. IV.

Figure 59
Unknown artist
British
Sarah Siddons (1755–1831) as Ophelia, c. 1785–1786
Pen and ink with brown wash
By Permission of the Folger Shakespeare Library

References

Altick, Richard. *Paintings from Books: Art and Literature in Britain, 1760–1900*. Columbus: Ohio State University Press, 1985.

An Actress. *The True Ophelia: and other studies of Shakespeare's Women*. London: Sidgwick, 1913.

Ashton, Geoffrey. *Shakespeare and British Art*. Exh. cat. Yale Center for British Art, New Haven, 1981.

Auerbach, Nina. *Romantic Imprisonment: Women and Other Glorified Outcasts*. New York: Columbia University Press, 1986.

Barber, Frances. "Ophelia in *Hamlet*." *Players of Shakespeare 2*. Eds. Russell Jackson and Robert Smallwood. Cambridge: Cambridge University Press, 1988.

Barthes, Roland. *Image, Music, Text*. Ed. and Trans. Stephen Heath. New York: The Noonday Press, 1977.

Bashkirtseff, Marie. "Journal posthume d'une artiste (Fragments). "*L'Artiste*. 1(jan., fév. 1887): 58–64; 122–131.

Branagh, Kenneth, ed. *Hamlet*, New York: W. W. Norton, 1996.

Brokoph-Mauch, Gudrun. "Salome and Ophelia: The Representation of Women in Fin-de-Siècle Austrian Literature." *Modern Austrian Literature*. 22. 3–4 (1989): 241–255.

Bronfen, Elisabeth. *Over Her Dead Body: Death, Femininity and the Aesthetic*. New York: Routledge, 1992.

Bronson, Betrand H., ed. *Samuel Johnson: 'Rasselas,' Poems, and Selected Prose*. New York: Holt, Rinehart and Winston, 1952.

Brustein, Robert. "Twenty-First Century *Hamlet*." *The New Republic* (18–25 July 1988): 28.

Bulman, James and H. R. Coursen, eds. *Shakespeare on Television*. Hanover: University of New England Press, 1988.

Coddon, Karin S. "'Suche Strange Dessygns': Madness, Subjectivity, and Treason in *Hamlet* and Elizabethan Culture." *Hamlet*. Ed. Susan L. Wofford. Boston: Bedford, 1994: 380–402.

Cohen, Michael. *'Hamlet': In My Mind's Eye*. Athens: University of Georgia Press, 1989.

Conolly, John. *A Study of Hamlet*. London: Edward Moxon & Co., 1863.

Cookson, Linda and Brian Loughrey, eds. *Hamlet*. London: Longman, 1988.

Coursen, H. R. *Christian Ritual and the World of Shakespeare's Tragedies*. Cranbury, New Jersey: Associated University Presses, 1978.

_____ . *A Jungian Approach to Shakespeare*. Washington: University Press of America, 1986.

_____ . "'Must There No More Be Done?: Images of Ophelia." *Shakespearean Performance as Interpretation*. Newark: University of Delaware Press, 1992.

_____ . *Shakespeare in Production: Whose History?* Athens: Ohio University Press, 1996.

_____ . "The Closet Scene." *Approaches to Teaching Shakespeare's 'Hamlet.'* Ed. Bernice W. Kliman. New York: Modern Language Association. Forthcoming, 2001.

_____ . *Shakespeare in Space: Recent Productions on Screen*. New York: Peter Lang, 2001.

Crowl, Samuel. "*Hamlet*: A Review of the Almereyda Production." *Shakespeare Bulletin*, forthcoming, 2001.

Davison, Peter. *Hamlet: Text & Performance*. London: Macmillan, 1983.

Dawson, Anthony. *Shakespeare in Performance: 'Hamlet.'* Manchester: Manchester University Press, 1995.

Dijkstra, Bram. *Idols of Perversity: Fantasies of Feminine Evil in Fin-de-Siècle Culture*. New York and Oxford: Oxford University Press, 1986.

Donaldson, Sandra M. "Ophelia in Elizabeth Siddal Rossetti's Poem 'A Year and a Day.'" *Journal of Pre-Raphaelite Studies* 2.1 (1981): 127–33.

Erdman, Jean. *Dance and Myth: The World of Jean Erdman. Part 1. The Early Dances*. Exec. Prod. Nancy Allison. New York: Mystic Fire Video, 1995.

Floyd-Wilson, Mary. "Ophelia and Femininity in the Eighteenth Century: 'Dangerous conjectures in ill-breeding minds,'" *Women's Studies*. 21 (1992): 397–409.

Fraser, R. Scott. "On Ophelia," *Shakespeare and the Visual Arts*. Eds. Klein, Holger and James L. Harner. Lewiston, Queenston, Lampeter: The Edwin Mellen Press, 2000. (*Shakespeare Yearbook* 11 [2000]) 238-259.

Frye, R. M. *The Renaissance 'Hamlet': Issues and Responses in 1600*. Princeton: Princeton University Press, 1984.

Gervinus, Georg Gottfried. *Shakespeare Commentaries*. Leipzig, 1849-50. Trans. F. E.Bunnett. London: Smith, Elder, 1883.

Gilman, Sander L., ed. *The Face of Madness, Hugh Diamond and the Origin of Psychiatric Photography*. New York: Brunner/Mazel, 1976.

Gorokhoff, Galina, ed. *Love Locked Out: The Memoirs of Anna Lea Merritt with a Checklist of Her Works*. Boston: Museum of Fine Arts, 1981.

Granville-Barker, Harley. *Preface to 'Hamlet.'* London: Nick Hern, 1993.

Greenblatt, Stephen, ed. *The Norton Shakespeare*. New York: W.W. Norton, 1997.

Gregory Crewdson: Dream of Life. Exh. cat. Salamanca: Ediciones Universidad de Salamanca, 1999.

Hancock, Nelson. "The Ultimate Film Still: The Art Photographer Gregory Crewdson Shares Tales from the Set of His Latest Production." *The New York Times Magazine*. March 25, 2001: 50–53.

Hapgood, Robert. "Shakespeare and the Included Spectator." *Reinterpretations of Renaissance Drama*. Ed. Norman Rabkin. New York: Columbia University Press, 1969: 117–36.

Hares–Stryker, Carolyn, ed. *An Anthology of Pre-Raphaelite Writings*. New York: New York University Press, 1997.

Hassel, R. Chris. "Painted Women: Annunciation Motifs in *Hamlet.*" *Comparative Drama* 32 (1998-99): 47–84.

Hibbard, G.R., ed. *Hamlet.* Oxford: Oxford University Press, 1987.

Holland, Peter. "*Hamlet:* Text in Performance." *Hamlet.* Eds. Peter J. Smith and Nigel Wood. Buckingham: Open University Press, 1996: 55–82.

Jameson, Anna. *Characteristics of Women, Moral, Poetical and Historical.* 1832. 3rd ed. 2 vols. London: Saunders and Otley, 1835.

Jenkins, Harold, ed. *Hamlet.* London: Methuen, 1982.

Klein, Holger and James L. Harner, eds. *Shakespeare and the Visual Arts.* Lewiston, Queenston, Lampeter: The Edwin Mellen Press, 2000. (*Shakespeare Yearbook* 11 [2000])

Knowles, Richard Paul. "The Real of It Would Be Awful: Representing the Real Ophelia in Canada." *Theatre Survey.* 39.1 (May 1998): 21–40.

Kozintsev, Grigori. *Shakespeare: Time and Conscience.* Trans. Joyce Vining. London: Dennis Dobson, 1967.

Leigh-Noel, Madeleine. *Shakspeare's Garden of Girls.* London: Remington, 1885.

Lewes, Louis. *The Women of Shakespeare.* Stuttgart, 1893. Trans. Helen Zimmern. New York: Putnam's; London: Hodder, 1895.

Lootens, Tricia. *Lost Saints: Silence, Gender, and Victorian Literary Canonization.* Charlottesville: University Press of Virginia, 1996.

Lusardi, James P. "*Hamlet IV.*" *Shakespeare Bulletin* 8. 2 (Spring 1990): 21–23.

Lyons, Bridget Gellert. "The Iconography of Ophelia." *ELH* 44 (1977): 60–74.

Marsh, Jan. *Pre-Raphaelite Women.* London: Artus, 1994.

Martin, Helena Faucit. *On Some of Shakespeare's Female Characters.* 1885. 5th ed. Edinburgh: Blackwood, 1893.

McLuskie, Kathleen. "The Patriarchal Bard." *Political Shakespeare.* Eds. Jonathan Dollimore and Alan Sinfield. Manchester: Manchester University Press, 1985.

Minogue, Valerie. "Rimbaud's *Ophelia,*" *French Studies: A Quarterly Review.* 43.4 (Oct. 1989): 423–436.

Nardo, Anna. "'Hamlet': A Man to Double Business Bound." *Shakespeare Quarterly* 34 (1983): 181–199.

Nicoletti, Lisa. "Resuscitating Ophelia : Images of Suicide and Suicidal Insanity in Nineteenth-Century England," Ph.D. diss. University of Wisconsin-Madison, 1999.

O'Donnell, Jessie Fremont. "Ophelia." *The American Shakespeare Magazine* 3 (March 1897): 70–6. Rpt. *Women Reading Shakespeare 1660–1900.* Eds. Ann Thompson and Sasha Roberts. Manchester and New York: Manchester University Press, 1997. 241–242.

Païni, Dominique and Guy Cogeval. *Hitchcock and Art: Fatal Coincidences.* Exh. cat. Montreal, Montreal Museum of Fine Arts, 2001.

Parsons, Keith and Pamela Mason, eds. *Shakespeare in Performance.* London: Salamander, 1995.

Patrick, Maria. Producer. "Egg Interview with Gregory Crewdson." *Egg: the arts show.* WNET/New York. http://www.pbs.org/wnet/egg. July 26, 2001.

Pennington, Michael. *Hamlet: A User's Guide.* New York: Limelight, 1996.

Peterson, Kaara. "Framing Ophelia: Representation and the Pictorial Tradition." *Mosaic* 31.3 (1998): 1–24. Rpt. *Shakespearean Criticism,* 48: Yearbook 1998. Detroit: Gale, 2000: 255–263.

Pipher, Mary. *Reviving Ophelia: Saving the Selves of Adolescent Girls.* New York: Ballantine Books, 1994.

Poulson, Christine. "Death and the Maiden: The Lady of Shalott and the Pre-Raphaelites." *Re-framing the Pre-Raphaelites: Historical and Theoretical Essays.* Ed. Ellen Harding. Aldershot, England; Brookfield, Vermont: Scolar Press, 1996.

Purkiss, Diane. *The Witch in History: Early Modern and Twentieth-Century Interpretations.* London: Routledge, 1996.

Raby, Peter. *'Fair Ophelia': A Life of Harriet Smithson Berlioz.* Cambridge: Cambridge University Press, 1982.

Rhodes, Kimberly. "Performing Roles: Images of Ophelia in Britain, 1740-1910," Ph.D. diss. Columbia University, 1999.

Rimbaud, Arthur. *Complete Works.* Trans. Paul Schmidt. New York: HarperPerennial, 2000.

Rosenberg, Marvin. *The Masks of 'Hamlet.'* Newark: University of Delaware Press, 1992.

Rossetti, William Michael. *Dante Gabriel Rossetti. His Family Letters with a Memoir.* 2 vols. London, 1895; New York: AMS, 1970.

Rothwell, Kenneth S. and Annabelle H. Melzer. *Shakespeare on Screen.* New York: Neal-Schuman, 1990.

Rozett, Martha Tuck. "Drowning Ophelias and Other Images of Death in Shakespeare's Plays." *Shakespeare and the Visual Arts.* Eds. Holger Klein and James Harner. Lewiston, Queenston, Lampeter: The Edwin Mellen Press, 2000. (*Shakespeare Yearbook* 11[2000]) 182–196.

Rusche, Harry. *Shakespeare Illustrated.* Emory University. http://www.emory.edu./ENGLISH/classes/Shakespeare_Illustrated.Shakespeare.html

Ruskin, John. "Of Queens' Gardens." *Sesame and Lilies.* 1865. London: Allen, 1904.

Schucking, Levin. *Character Problems in Shakespeare's Plays.* Berlin, 1917. English Translation, New York, 1922.

Scolnicov, Hanna. "Intertextuality and Realism in Three Versions of *Hamlet*: The Willow Speech and the Aesthetics of Cinema," *Shakespeare and the Visual Arts.* Eds. Holger Klein and James Harner. Lewiston, Queenston, Lampeter: The Edwin Mellen Press, 2000. (*Shakespeare Yearbook* 11 [2000]) 227–237.

Shandler, Nina. *Ophelia's Mom: Women Speak Out about Loving and Letting Go of Their Adolescent Daughters.* New York: Crown Publishers, 2001.

Shandler, Sara. *Ophelia Speaks: Adolescent Girls Write about Their Search for Self.* New York: Harper Collins, 1999.

Shattuck, Charles H. *Shakespeare on the American Stage.* II. Cranbury, New Jersey: Associated University Presses, 1987.

Showalter, Elaine. *The Female Malady: Women, Madness and English Culture, 1830–1980*. New York: Pantheon Books, 1985.

_____ . "Representing Ophelia: Women, Madness, and the Responsibilities of Feminist Criticism." *Shakespeare and the Question of Theory*. Eds. Patricia Parker and Geoffrey Hartman. New York: Methuen, 1985. 77–94.

Siegfried, B. R. "Ethics, Interpretation, and Shakespeare's Ophelia: The Re-emergence of Visual Phronesis in the Works of Maclise, Rossetti, Préault, and Abbey," *Shakespeare and the Visual Arts*. Eds. Holger Klein and James Harner. Lewiston, Queenston, Lampeter: The Edwin Mellen Press, 2000. (*Shakespeare Yearbook* 11 [2000]) 197–226.

Smith, Carol. *Louise Bourgeois Prints: 1989–1998*. Exh. cat. Maier Museum of Art, Randolph-Macon Woman's College, Lynchburg, Virginia, 1999.

States, Bert O. *Hamlet and the Concept of Character.* Baltimore: Johns Hopkins University Press, 1992.

Steichen, Edward. *A Life in Photography*. Garden City, New York: Doubleday & Co., 1963.

Stern, Jeffrey. "Lewis Carroll the Pre-Raphaelite 'Fainting in Coils.'" *Lewis Carroll Observed*. Ed. Edward Guiliano. NY: Potter, 1976. 161–180.

Stubbs, Laura. "That Shakespeare's Women Are Ideals." *The Stratford-upon-Avon Herald*, July 1898. 246–249.

Terry, Ellen. *The Story of My Life*. New York: Schocken Books, 1982.

Thomas, Sidney. *The Antic Hamlet and Richard III.* London: King Crown's Press, 1943.

Thompson, Ann and Sasha Roberts, eds. *Women Reading Shakespeare 1660–1900*. Manchester and New York: Manchester University Press, 1997.

Trewin, J. C. *Five and Eighty Hamlets*. London: Hutchinson, 1987.

Updike, John. *Gertrude and Claudius*. New York: Knopf, 1998.

Vest, James. M. *The French Face of Ophelia from Belleforest to Baudelaire*. Lanham, New York and London: University Press of America, 1989.

_____ . "Reflections of Ophelia (and of Hamlet) in Alfred Hitchcock's *Vertigo*." *Journal of the Midwest Modern Language Association*. 22 (1986): 1–9.

Victor Burgin. Essays by Peter Wollen, Francette Pacteau, Norman Bryson. Exh. cat. Fundació Antonio Tàpies, Barcelona, 2001.

West, Rebecca. *The Court and the Castle*. New Haven: Yale University Press, 1947.

Wollen, Peter. "Barthes, Burgin, *Vertigo*," *Victor Burgin*. exh. cat. Fundació Antonio Tàpies, Barcelona, 2001. 10–26.

Young, Alan R. "Hamlet and Nineteenth-Century Photography," *Shakespeare and theVisual Arts*. Eds. Holger Klein and James Harner. Lewiston, Queenston, Lampeter: The Edwin Mellen Press, 2000. (*Shakespeare Yearbook* 11 [2000]) 260–307.

Ziegler, Georgianna, ed., with Frances E. Dolan and Jeanne Addison Roberts. *Shakespeare's Unruly Women*. Exh. cat. Folger Shakespeare Library, Washington, D.C., 1997.

Figure 60
JOHN AUSTEN
Death of Ophelia, 1922
Pen and ink
By Permission of the Folger Shakespeare Library

Index of Artists

Figure 61
(Joseph) Kenny Meadows
Untitled [The Death of Ophelia], 1846
Wood engraving
By Permission of the Folger Shakespeare Library